Cambridge Elements

Elements in International Relations
edited by
Jon C. W. Pevehouse
University of Wisconsin–Madison
Tanja A. Börzel
Freie Universität Berlin
Edward D. Mansfield
University of Pennsylvania

NORMS, PRACTICES, AND SOCIAL CHANGE IN GLOBAL POLITICS

Steven Bernstein
University of Toronto

Aarie Glas
Northern Illinois University

Marion Laurence
Dalhousie University

Shaftesbury Road, Cambridge CB2 8EA, United Kingdom

One Liberty Plaza, 20th Floor, New York, NY 10006, USA

477 Williamstown Road, Port Melbourne, VIC 3207, Australia

314–321, 3rd Floor, Plot 3, Splendor Forum, Jasola District Centre, New Delhi – 110025, India

103 Penang Road, #05–06/07, Visioncrest Commercial, Singapore 238467

Cambridge University Press is part of Cambridge University Press & Assessment, a department of the University of Cambridge.

We share the University's mission to contribute to society through the pursuit of education, learning and research at the highest international levels of excellence.

www.cambridge.org
Information on this title: www.cambridge.org/9781009561013

DOI: 10.1017/9781009560986

© Steven Bernstein, Aarie Glas and Marion Laurence 2025

This publication is in copyright. Subject to statutory exception and to the provisions of relevant collective licensing agreements, with the exception of the Creative Commons version the link for which is provided below, no reproduction of any part may take place without the written permission of Cambridge University Press & Assessment.

An online version of this work is published at doi.org/10.1017/9781009560986 under a Creative Commons Open Access license CC-BY-NC 4.0 which permits re-use, distribution and reproduction in any medium for non-commercial purposes providing appropriate credit to the original work is given and any changes made are indicated. To view a copy of this license visit https://creativecommons.org/licenses/by-nc/4.0

When citing this work, please include a reference to the DOI 10.1017/9781009560986

First published 2025

A catalogue record for this publication is available from the British Library

ISBN 978-1-009-56101-3 Hardback
ISBN 978-1-009-56099-3 Paperback
ISSN 2515-706X (online)
ISSN 2515-7302 (print)

Cambridge University Press & Assessment has no responsibility for the persistence or accuracy of URLs for external or third-party internet websites referred to in this publication and does not guarantee that any content on such websites is, or will remain, accurate or appropriate.

For EU product safety concerns, contact us at Calle de José Abascal, 56, 1°, 28003 Madrid, Spain, or email eugpsr@cambridge.org

Norms, Practices, and Social Change in Global Politics

Elements in International Relations

DOI: 10.1017/9781009560986
First published online: March 2025

Steven Bernstein
University of Toronto

Aarie Glas
Northern Illinois University

Marion Laurence
Dalhousie University

Author for correspondence: Aarie Glas, aglas@niu.edu

Abstract: Debate over how to recognize and understand change and continuity has long animated the field of International Relations. This Element brings norm-oriented and practice-oriented approaches into conversation to advance a wide-ranging account of change and continuity in global politics. It elaborates four scenarios in which norm and practice interactions produce change and continuity: relative continuity and a tight coupling of practices and norms; change through accidental incompetence; new competencies that create disjunctures; and change through deliberate contestation. It demonstrates the utility of the approach using empirical illustrations from the fields of global health and development. The Element also shows the wider applicability of the scenarios for major contemporary debates about change in global governance and security. This title is also available as Open Access on Cambridge Core.

Keywords: norms, social change, global governance, international practices, international change

© Steven Bernstein, Aarie Glas and Marion Laurence 2025

ISBNs: 9781009561013 (HB), 9781009560993 (PB), 9781009560986 (OC)
ISSNs: 2515-706X (online), 2515-7302 (print)

Contents

1 Introduction 1

2 Debating Change 15

3 Four Analytical Scenarios of Social Change 26

4 Applications 35

5 Conclusion 50

 References 62

1 Introduction

Debate over how to recognize and understand patterns of change and continuity has long animated the field of International Relations (IR). The focus of these debates varies considerably: the rise and fall of great powers; the onset of war and attempts at lasting peace; the emergence and effects of new ideas, actors, and modes of governance on relations among political units, across their boundaries, or that transcend them; changes in global orders or systems; or even a focus on relationships between human and natural systems that acknowledges enmeshment of "rapid and far-reaching processes of change in technology, climate, demography, science, [and] modes of production and communication" (Flockhart 2022: 25).

This Element begins with a bold claim that underpinning nearly all of these debates is a shared understanding of meaningful change as social and relational. In other words, in IR, what separates continuity from meaningful change is when political identities and practices take new forms, when patterns of behaviour emerge that were not previously comprehensible, or when prevailing formal and informal rules seem no longer to apply or are replaced by alternatives. We unpack further what we mean by social and relational below, but a simple and well-known example makes our point. When the Cold War ended, the resurgence of debates about "change" focused less on the material fact of the new balance of power than on whether the collapse of the Soviet Union signalled a shift in the world order, expectations of more peaceful interaction, or the "triumph" and diffusion of liberalism. Even realist IR theory, with its emphasis on continuity and skepticism of fundamental change, understands major change primarily through the lens of changes in actor identities (system change), governance arrangements, or interactions (Gilpin 1981; Mearsheimer 2019). Meanwhile, much of the contemporary scholarship on change concerns the more everyday responses to global challenges that affect people's lives – from climate change and health emergencies like pandemics to human rights and inequality (McNamara and Newman 2020; Newell et al. 2021; Bernstein 2024), or the underlying challenges to, or reproductions of, liberal (e.g., Lake, Martin, and Risse 2021; Goddard et al. 2024) or racialized orders (Zvobgo and Loken 2020) – and whether they alter or reproduce existing practices and behaviours.

Two contemporary strands of IR scholarship that most directly address social change are constructivist literatures that highlight *norms* as the underpinnings of social order, and the growing scholarship on *international practices*. The former highlights how new or evolving norms constitute change while the latter focuses on the "how" or performance of continuity and change. Unfortunately, these theoretical camps are often siloed in the discipline, and in some cases are overtly critical of the other on both theoretical and empirical grounds. We eschew this opposition. Not only do we find value in both theoretical literatures, but we also argue that norms and practices – and how they interact – are essential for understanding patterns of change and continuity in global politics. Hence, in this Element, we bring norm-oriented and practice-oriented approaches into conversation to advance a comprehensive and general account of change and continuity in global politics.

In effect, then, our purpose is twofold: to introduce a new way to understand patterns of change and continuity in global politics and to contribute to a better understanding of these two strands of IR theory and how they can productively be brought into dialogue. Via this dialogue, our key contribution is to develop a framework that provides the analytic scaffolding to account for patterns and processes of change to demonstrate its utility for empirical research.

To be clear, our account does not dispute the myriad possible sources and causes of change that animate debates in the IR and global politics fields – including but not limited to great power rivalry, new technologies or techniques of warfare from nuclear weapons to hybrid warfare and its various components including cyberwarfare, other communication and technological innovations in multiple sectors, novel or shifting modes of governance or legitimacy crises, new economic and political actors or forms of collective action, increasing density or complexity of transactions or interdependence, or external and sometimes non-human shocks or crises. Rather, while acknowledging the many possible and complex sources and causes of change, we show how this scholarship can be strengthened by a focus on the relations between norms and practices precisely because the visible manifestation and recognition of change in global politics and relations is experienced and understood through the lens of social change, even as change is buffeted by a wide variety of internal (to agents) and external factors. Indeed, we are agnostic on the ultimate causes of normative change and practice change. However, like Flockhart (2016, 2022), we believe it is productive to operate through a relational lens in order to understand, observe, and analyze the social change that nearly all of IR theory recognizes as meaningful and significant.

To these ends, our approach builds on and extends a growing literature attentive – implicitly, and increasingly explicitly – to interactions and relationships between norms and practice (e.g., Bode and Huelss 2018; Wiener 2018; Bode and Karlsrud 2019; Bernstein and Laurence 2022; Glas and Laurence 2022; Pratt 2022; Lesch and Loh 2022; Bode 2024; Bouris and Fernández-Molina 2024). Taking this growing literature a step further, we develop an original framework to analyze the variable interplay between norms and practices to systemically showcase the different pathways by which this interaction produces change and continuity. Through this strategy, we identify four scenarios that reflect a wide range of possibilities for patterns of continuity and change of interest to IR scholars: relative continuity that rests on the tight coupling of practices and norms; change through "accidental incompetence" or unintentional change that creates new patterns of action; new competencies, deliberate shifts in practice, or normative change that create disjunctures between practices and norms; and social change through deliberate contestation. In doing so, we demonstrate plausible pathways—and empirical strategies to investigate them—to make sense of supposed changes in global politics.

While most extant literature focuses on the first and the last scenarios, in this Element we systematically describe a fuller range of scenarios, thereby providing the analytic tools for scholars to understand and empirically investigate social change in more nuanced and productive ways. In doing so, we make novel contributions to the literature on change by taking relational and practice-based critiques of the norms literature seriously, while preserving the concept of a "norm" – a concept that still holds analytical value, and one that has significant resonance among practitioners themselves, many of whom use it to make sense of their own actions and the world around them (Glas and Laurence 2022, 5).

To get us there, we guide readers through the debates between the two dominant strands of social theorizing in IR and demonstrate how such a conversation produces a more productive understanding of change than adopting either conceptual approach in isolation, as has long been the case. We then provide several examples that illustrate our scenarios of change in action to demonstrate the analytical utility of this more nuanced approach to accounting for change and continuity.

In the remainder of this Introduction, we further unpack our understanding of international change as primarily social and relational. We then elaborate on why a focus on the interaction of norms and practices is an especially productive way forward to analyze and understand change in global politics. We close by outlining the plan of this Element.

International Change: Social and Relational

Whereas a growing literature is attentive to the dynamics of both stability and change in international or global social relations, how to define or empirically recognize "change" remains debated. In this Element, we understand social change as modifications to behaviour including speech and rhetoric and/or the formal and informal rules that govern behaviour. As we demonstrate, modifications in behaviour need not follow modifications in rules. Our dual focus aligns with statements from scholars who have suggested social change refers to both modifications in how "one goes on in the world" and to the "social facts" that influence global politics more generally (Searle 1995; Ruggie 1998; Hopf 2018, 692). We see evidence of dynamics of social change in variable patterns of identities and empowerment of various agents, their actions and through alterations in rhetorical and discursive acts.

Put another way, our interest is in changes in practice (i.e., the meaningful performances enacted rather unreflexively by communities as patterns of actions) and/or norms that comprise the institutional basis of global politics and orders. Here we find Finnemore and Sikkink's (1998) understanding of institutions particularly insightful. It highlights that, while institutions may define and regulate international interactions, practically speaking they are collections of norms and practices, and it is therefore through their relationships that we must ultimately look to understand and analyze continuity and change.[1] In other words, social change is best understood relationally. It occurs through processes or shifting transactional contexts that reproduce or transform the structural environments in which they are enmeshed, as opposed to via political actors with fixed identities who simply cause or react to background conditions (Emirbayer 1997; Kurki 2022; Flockhart 2022).

Others have similarly noted the value of adopting a relational ontology, especially to account for changes in the fast-moving and increasingly complex environment of contemporary global politics. Flockhart (2022, 32), for example, recognizes "change as both an emergent phenomenon involving a myriad of intentional and habitual actions, unintended consequences, random events and the many intra- and inter-actions that change us, [which] requires [scholars to adopt] a relational and holistic approach that can encompass the multiplicity of global life." However, recognizing the value of a relational ontology for understanding and analyzing change is only a first step. Its great advantage is that from it, we can observe different combinations and interactions of intentional and habitual actions. From there, however, theory development is needed to guide analysts on where to look for, and how to analyze and understand patterns of change and continuity that reflect these interactions. We do so by developing scenarios around several of those combinations, focusing on the interactions of norms and practices, to unpack and systematically analyze different processes through which change occurs. Our approach requires

---

[1] This differs from March and Olsen (1998, 948), for example, who define an institution as a "relatively stable collection of practices and rules defining appropriate behaviour for specific groups of actors in specific situations," a definition that locates norms, practices, and institutions under a single conceptual umbrella.

differentiating norms from practice. This is a key *analytical* move for our framework that allows us to identify processes that generate change that otherwise would not be visible.

One by-product of the historical bifurcation between norm- and practice-oriented approaches is a tendency among scholars to subsume their less-favoured concept – either norms or practice – within their preferred concept. There are compelling theoretical reasons for doing so. Indeed, norms can be subsumed within the concept of competent practice (a recognition of competence being requisite upon agreed understandings of effective and/or appropriate conduct) and practices can be subsumed within norms (given that norms speak to appropriate conduct, enactments that align with common conceptions of "practice"). We argue, however, that drawing an analytical distinction between norms and practice is useful for anchoring empirical research on social change in global politics. This distinction makes visible how each can evolve independently and how their interaction and relationship over time produce various patterns and processes of change.

So far, we have discussed change as if it is self-evident. Extensive debates in the field suggest it is anything but, which is perhaps unsurprising given that we have just argued for its social and relational character. Whereas Section 2 explores these debates around change in more detail, as a starting point, we outline three basic epistemological and conceptual distinctions we adopt to identify and study change.

First, observing change is inherently perspective-dependent. For example, scholars and other outside observers may see meaningful changes in behaviours and rules, while those enacting these behaviours and bound by these rules may attest to continuity. UN peace operations over time are a good illustration. Most external observers of UN peacekeeping would see marked and important differences in both mandate and practice, ranging from the rules on when and how to use force to peacekeepers' role in peacebuilding and the extension of state authority amid conflict. Meanwhile, practitioners within this context often attest to continuity in both rules and behaviour over time, especially regarding the underpinning norm of impartiality, even when new patterns of action depart significantly from traditional peacekeeping practice (see Laurence 2019, 2024b). Put differently, the realness and tangibility of a change may be contested and understood differently based on varied situatedness. The nature and direction of change can also be up for debate, and change will typically defy binary conceptions of stability versus change or proponents of change versus opponents (e.g., Jütersonke et al. 2021, 947). For instance, the concept of state sovereignty has evolved significantly since its mythic pronouncement in 1648, even if the meaning of new rules and behaviours is complex and debated (e.g., compare Krasner 1999 to Biersteker and Weber 1996). Such disagreements and contestation do not, however, undermine the observability of meaningful change. Other examples include decolonization and the women's suffrage movement, both of which clearly produced meaningful alterations in practices and institutions in global politics, even if their impact on specific individuals and communities has varied widely. Our account of social change, then, begins from an external analytical perspective – how we as scholars observe and make sense of changes that we perceive in practice and institutions.

Second, modifications in behaviour need not lead to modifications in formal rules to be recognized as change, as we addressed above. Here the distinction between practices, norms and institutions is critical, with the latter being composed of clusters of both norms and practices (Finnemore and Sikkink 1998, 891). This aggregation, and the resulting interrelationships, mean that change in a single norm or practice does not necessarily yield immediate changes across other components of an institution. For example, both the Hague Convention of 1907 and the UN Charter suggest that states engaged in war ought to declare it. Since the Second World War, however, the practice of formally declaring war has fallen by the wayside. At the same time, we have not seen accompanying changes in formal international rules around declarations of war (see Pullen and Frost 2022). Conversely, new or altered rules may not evidence modifications of practice itself. The 1928 Kellogg–Briand Pact outlawing war is perhaps the most infamous example (though even in this case, one might argue that it laid the groundwork for practice change and normative change in the ways wars are justified, for example, the need to invoke self-defence and strong norms against aggression). Even in cases when formal norms become widely accepted, behaviours contrary to those norms may persist. For example, Rosenberg (2022) demonstrates empirically that despite a widespread end to race-based immigration policies in the latter half of the twentieth century, racial bias in international migration persists.

Third, we centre our attention on the dynamics of change within and around formal governance institutions, including examining the behaviours of states and other agents within and beyond international organizations. However, as we posit in the conclusion, our analysis of social change speaks to dynamics beyond state agents and institutionalized settings as well, including how social agents and communities of all kinds enact, understand, contest, and reject principles and practices. Within the context of governance institutions, we show that change is often driven by contestation over what is understood as the correct, appropriate, or effective way to "get things done": the norms of different communities and their enactment in practice. Thus, our account of social change in this Element draws on literatures that examine both norms and practices in IR and can be applied across a range of institutionalized and non-institutionalized settings.

Practices and Norms: A Productive Encounter to Understand Change

Across existing treatments, norms are generally understood as social facts with prescriptive and constitutive qualities recognized as such by a discrete community of actors (Jurkovich 2020). Practices generally refer to socially meaningful performances, enacted largely as matter of course or unreflexively by groups of actors (Adler and Pouliot 2011). Both concepts, then, speak to potentially important aspects of stability and change in social relations and a rich literature undergirds contemporary treatments. The literature on norms has traditionally centred on accounting for change in global politics. Pioneering work explored how new norms emerge, diffuse, and are institutionalized, shaping the behaviour of states and other actors in meaningful ways (e.g., Keck and Sikkink 1998) and how existing norms spread and change as they are made to fit with established understandings of appropriateness or efficacy (e.g., Bernstein 2001; Acharya 2004). Practice theory, on the other hand, has largely been adopted to explain continuity in social relations, particularly in reference to governance behaviours of states and communities of state officials (e.g., Pouliot 2010; Davies 2016). Indeed, a pervasive critique of practice theorizing is its lack of attention to change (Duvall and Chowdhury 2011; Bueger and Gadinger 2014; Schindler and Willes 2015; Hopf 2018). The growing literature that places these conceptual foci in dialogue has aimed to uncover the analytical importance of the practice of norms for social change. Yet, these dynamics of change remain much debated.

To arrive at our account of change and continuity in global politics we start with the literature on international practices (e.g., Adler and Pouliot 2011; Bueger and Gadinger 2015; Drieschova, Bueger, and Hopf 2022). This scholarship tends to explore both continuity and change by centring analytical attention on the minutiae of international interactions between and within communities of people, interactions that produce stability in the complex social and political world and that carry with them the potential for change. In most accounts, stability and the potential for change emerge largely from taken-for-granted knowledge and meaningful patterns of action that flow from it. In this way, accounts of practices often speak to similar questions and offer similar analyses as accounts of global politics centred on institutions, norms, or collective expectations regarding appropriate conduct (Katzenstein 1996; Jurkovich

2020). Indeed, according to proponents, one of practice theory's strengths is its versatility; it can be used to make sense of stability and change across a variety of institutional settings and beyond (Adler and Pouliot 2011, 17–18). It can also be used to study institutions themselves, which are understood as being composed of "bundles" of practices. Practices, perform the "legwork" that sets institutions in motion and "sustain[s] their existence at the level of action" (Pouliot 2020, 745).

Here we see not only an important point of contact, but also some conceptual conflation, where each group of scholars speaks of institutions in similar ways, but substitutes "practices" and "norms" when identifying the components that constitute institutions. Yet, implied in the definition of institutions above by a prominent practice theorist (Pouliot 2020) is already an idea of an institution's stable "existence," suggesting they are also composed of norms or stable expectations.

Indeed – and perhaps surprisingly to scholars in both traditions – practice-based accounts of institutions like the one above are remarkably similar to the classic characterization of institutions by the two most prominent norms theorists, Martha Finnemore and Kathryn Sikkink. Their classic 1998 article on the norm "life cycle" highlights the common error of equating a norm with an institution:

> The danger in using the norm language is that it can obscure distinct and interrelated elements of social institutions if not used carefully. For example, political scientists tend to slip into discussions of 'sovereignty' or 'slavery' as if they were norms, when in fact they are (or were) collections of norms and the mix of *rules and practices* [emphasis added] that structure these institutions has varied significantly over time. Used carefully, however, norm language can help to steer scholars toward looking inside social institutions and considering the components of social institutions as well as the way these elements are renegotiated into new arrangements over time to create new patterns of politics. (1998, 891)

However, recognizing this dual constitution of institutions as bundles of norms and practices begs – but does not address – the question our framework illuminates: how and in what ways do these bundles of relationships lead to change and continuity? Our different scenarios are designed to capture when norms and practices are, for example, mutually reinforcing or in a relationship of positive feedback (scenario 1) or when their motion leads to disjuncture and hypocrisy (scenario 3). Our approach, then, allows researchers to unpack and analyze what the institutionalist literature has long recognized: collections of practices and rules or norms need not perfectly align to be stable, yet it is precisely those relationships that help us understand endogenous sources of continuity and change.

A prominent example in the constructivist norms literature nicely illustrates this point. In 1982, John Ruggie famously identified a bundle of norms[2] that underpinned major post-war economic institutions wherein the multilateral liberal economic order was predicated on various forms of domestic intervention or public management of domestic economies. The specific norms governing international trade and finance, as embodied in the GATT and the Bretton Woods institutions until they started to break down in the early 1970s, underpinned these relatively stable institutions even as practices varied considerably both before and after the end of the fixed exchange rate regime (e.g., Helleiner 2019). Identifying a set of norms and institutional arrangements can usefully reveal the underlying pattern of values and goals (what Ruggie called legitimate "social purposes") to which actors refer as authorizing or legitimizing international behaviour, and thus be a baseline for assessing change. Ruggie (1982, 384) made much of trying to differentiate "norm-governed" from "norm-transforming" change that followed in the post-Bretton Woods era. From a norms perspective, that is the end of the story.

Yet, Ruggie, among many other political economists, highlighted that after 1973, and even before, the practices of embedded liberalism rarely matched the normative ideal. A focus only on whether such changes were "norm-governed" or "norm transforming" severely limits our ability to see and analyze the changes. Broadening our perspective relationally and to include practices brings into view the real-time interplay of normative alternatives, sometimes existing simultaneously with the dominant institutional arrangements, as well as practices that actors and analysts have variously interpreted as norm consistent or norm challenging (Helleiner 2019). Our goal here is not to wade into this substantive debate, but to highlight both the value and irony of Ruggie's analysis. On the one hand, once identified and institutionalized, a norm-complex or institutionalized sets of norms can be used to assess the significance of changes in relation to underlying collective purposes. On the other hand, that is only half the story: missing from his norms-based analysis is a way to recognize and foreground practice changes that occur in constant motion and that interact with institutions, a dynamic that falls out of sight if they are defined and understood only through their normative constitution.

Ironically, Ruggie anticipated this very problem in his famous 1982 article, the last three pages of which (1982, 413–415) detail a range of practices that challenged the historic compromise – specifically "modes of externalization" of

---

[2] What elsewhere one of us has called a "norm-complex" (Bernstein 2001).

economic adjustment he observed at the time that, among things, shifted the burden of economic adjustment to open markets to developing countries by forcing liberalization and gutting public authority and fiscal space through privatization. On the one hand, this led Ruggie to make the argument in later work (e.g., Ruggie 1997, 2007) that the extreme versions of laissez-faire liberalism he observed in the 1990s posed a greater challenge to post-war economic regimes than many forms of protectionism. On the other hand, despite his explicit focus on the tensions these evolving practices created with the normative compromise of embedded liberalism, the analytic focus on "norm" governed versus transforming change severely truncates scholars' ability to observe, analyze, or assess the arguably massive and varied changes underway then or now (e.g., Helleiner 2019; Petersmann 2020; Mansfield and Rudra 2021; Kirshner 2024). A coherent theoretical framework is lacking to assess their significance or whether they will force new authoritative arrangements (in this case of state power and legitimate social purposes) or continue to exist in tension with existing formal arrangements.

Similarly, whereas Finnemore and Sikkink usefully recognized that institutions comprise norms *and* practices, their solution in their 1998 article was to analyze change by treating norms as the only relevant "component" of institutions. The remainder of their analysis then focused on the "life cycle" of that particular "component." Practices simply dropped out, as they do in much of the norms-based scholarship. Our framework brings practices back in, focusing on the analysis of their inter-relationships and their relationships with norms to understand patterns of continuity or stability and change.

Sovereignty, an example Finnemore and Sikkink highlighted themselves, is a paradigmatic example to illustrate this line of thinking. Krasner (1999), among many others, identified sovereignty as a relatively stable or slowly evolving set of norms bundled with a dynamic set of practices. Analyzing sovereignty as one or the other – norms *or* practices – would severely truncate our ability to understand changes in the institution of sovereignty and, indeed, of the state system. At the same time, to say norms of sovereignty "don't exist" would be unhelpful, even patently incorrect – they hold the constitutional status that has endured and is reinforced in the UN Charter, international law both in its rules and many of its practices, practices of international institutions in terms of standing and representation, diplomacy, and many other arrangements of the international system and society. And, yet, sovereignty practices are frequently in motion, sometimes reinforcing and sometimes in tension with sovereignty norms, with varying degrees of hypocrisy and overt contestation. For example, Schmidt's (2014, 817) analysis of "sovereign basing" – defined as the long-term peacetime presence of one state's military on another sovereign state's territory – demonstrates how shifting practices can be in tension with, and eventually transform, longstanding sovereignty norms. Only a framework that acknowledges both norms and practices can analyze and understand their interaction and changes or transformations in sovereignty that have been at the centre of debates in IR over order and system change (e.g., Bull 1977; Spruyt 1994; Bartelson 1995; Biersteker and Weber 1996; Krasner 1999; Flockhart 2022). The real-time conflict over Greenland playing out as we are going to press in early 2025, in the early days of US President Donald Trump's second term, is a perfect example of the importance of attention to norms and practices in understanding change, in precisely this context.

We also push back against practice theorists whose solution is adopting a pure relational ontology that collapses all social processes/entities under one conceptual umbrella (e.g., Pratt 2022; Lesch and Loh 2022). Doing so may mask dynamic processes of interaction and relations that otherwise help us see and understand significant change. In our view, such ontological purity is the enemy of analytic utility. To continue with the sovereignty example, only the relationship between norms of sovereignty and practices of imperialism, nationalism, resistance, and self-determination can help us see and understand the massive changes brought on by decolonization, even as norms of sovereignty and sovereign equality remained relatively constant throughout.

Other practice theorists take an opposite tack, proposing overly sharp analytic differences between norm-based, institution-based, and practice-based approaches. Adler and Pouliot (2011), in their influential volume making the case for practice-based approaches in the study of global politics, are careful to distinguish practices from norms. Practical knowledge from which practices unfold is "oriented toward action and, as such, it often resembles skill much more than the type of knowledge that can be brandished or represented, such as norms or ideas" (Adler and Pouliot 2011, 8). Others similarly argue that practice theories are separate from – and even directly opposed to – "norm-based constructivism," with its focus on processes such as socialization to norms or self-reflective discursive or collective action to contest or introduce new norms (Bueger and Gadinger 2015, 458; see also Weber 2020).

These sharp, sometimes contentious, distinctions arguably reflect the sociology of the discipline as much as they reflect substantive theoretical disagreements. Many early constructivists heavily emphasized practices and drew on much of the same intellectual material that now underpins practice theory. Over time, though, the field narrowed, and constructivism became closely associated with the study of norms, culture, and identity (McCourt 2016, 475, 481). In particular, attention to the emergence and contestation of international norms has become the mainstay of constructivist approaches to global politics. So robust is the literature on norms that some suggest norm research has become "an established sub-field" over time (Orchard and Wiener 2024). At the same time, despite many shared interests, practice theorists have eschewed a focus on norms. Rather, practice theorists in the early 2010s centred attention on carving out new intellectual space attentive not to the normative terrain of action, but to the "doing" itself or "the quotidian unfolding of international life" (Adler and Pouliot 2011, 3) and thus to developing lines of inquiry distinct from norm-based theorizing. Since these developments, norm-oriented scholars have been slow to engage with critical insights from practice theory, even though many conceptualize the significance and impact of norms in terms of practice (Betts and Orchard 2014, 2). This penchant for rigid distinctions led, initially, to the siloing of these two sets of literature within the field of IR, militating against potentially productive dialogue between them.

That early rigid bifurcation shows signs of softening. Increasingly we see efforts to explore the relationship between norms and practices, and to put norm-based approaches and practice-based approaches in fruitful conversation (e.g., Bode and Huelss 2018; Bernstein and Laurence 2022; Glas and Laurence 2022; Gadinger 2022; Pratt 2022; Lesch and Loh 2022; Bode 2024; Bouris and Fernández-Molina 2024; Laurence 2024b). This is a positive development as it widens IR scholars' conceptual toolkit. Given that both approaches are often used to explain the same empirical phenomena (Bourbeau 2017, 179), that dialogue has yielded important and novel insights into an array of important changes in global politics including the rise of protection of civilian mandates in UN peace operations, alterations in models of regional governance in Southeast Asia and East Africa, and changes in US security policies (Bode and Karlsrud 2019; Glas and Balogun 2020; Pratt 2022).

Similarly, many scholars develop more implicit dialogue between norms and practice to examine contestation and change across an array of areas. Nair, for example, shows how micro-level, quotidian practices of face-saving between the elite diplomats of the Association of Southeast Asian Nations (ASEAN) both generate group identity and make possible the normative terrain of ASEAN as an institution, including its preference for "conflict avoidance via a structure of iterative, informal, and discreet face-to-face interactions rather than legal instruments" (Nair 2019, 3). In her recent exploration of the crises of the liberal international order, Adler-Nissen develops a sociology of knowledge perspective to articulate the manifold ways in which the liberal international order is changing, less through the overt replacement of existing norms nor explicit contestation of normativity, but in and through practice that normalizes contestation (Adler-Nissen 2024, 2).

How much further might similar analyses go by explicitly drawing attention to the relative normative stability of institutional arrangements in interaction with practice change – as opposed to simply seeing contestation when the puzzle to be addressed is disjuncture of relative normative stability despite meaningful changes in practice? Such a move also enables investigation of the implications of those disjunctures for social change more broadly. In a recent special issue on communities of practice (CoP) in world politics, Adler, Bremberg, and Sondarjee (2024, 3) directly acknowledge these relations. They describe CoPs as "instruments for cultivating global governance's norms, values, and practices from the bottom up" (2024, 3). In the same issue, Bode (2024, 1) answers their call for more research examining the normativity of practice with her work on how CoPs shape normative debates about the appropriate use of lethal autonomous weapons systems.

These examples are part of a growing literature that implicitly and explicitly places norms and practice in dialogue to account for varied dynamics of change and contestation in global politics. Within this expanding literature, we see several important commonalities, and some important differences, and ensuing debates among these literatures on change and continuity. We systematically mine those debates in Section 2 to advance our own more general account of social change in global politics.

Centrally, we argue that identifying the varied interplay between norms and practice – dynamics that scholarship from each camp often overlooks – is a productive research direction to explain patterns of change and continuity in global politics. While we see initial steps in this direction in some recent works (e.g., Drieschova, Bueger, and Hopf 2022; Bouris and Fernández-Molina 2024), our analysis advances this scholarship by offering a fuller and more systematic appraisal of the relationships scholars have observed between norms and practices and how these differing relationships variably inform change.

Specifically, our analysis articulates four pathways, or analytical "scenarios," of change. Each scenario highlights variations in the relationship between norms and practices that produce different types and modes of social change. Depending on the relationship between norms and practices, each scenario speaks to relative continuity or relative change. In the first scenario, practices and norms are "tightly coupled," which produces significant overlap between standards for judging competence and shared beliefs about appropriateness. While neither norms nor practices are ever completely static, this scenario captures situations where congruence between norms and practices is conducive to relative continuity through positive feedback and mutual reinforcement. In a second scenario, change occurs through "accidental incompetence," when actors do not intend to contest the normative quality of behaviours but inadvertently do so. They thereby foster new patterns of action. Third, change may occur when new ways of being competent create a stark disjuncture or decoupling between practice and norm, but without overt acknowledgement or deliberate normative contestation. Conversely, normative change previously "entangled" with mutually reinforcing practice change may instead occur while practices remain unaltered (Bouris and Fernández-Molina 2024). One question this kind of change raises – though we cannot answer it fully here – is under what conditions such disjunctures will pull toward congruence, demanding new authoritative arrangements or relations. Finally, change may occur through active attempts to contest or reject norms through purposive contestation. In explicating each of the four scenarios, we draw on ongoing debates in the literature on norms and practice to highlight in each scenario the varied relationships between norms and practice, the role of agency and deliberative action, the conditions under which they are likely to occur, and how we might recognize the scope of change.

Our framework's contributions are not just theoretical; they are also methodological. By systematically identifying these four distinct scenarios and pathways by which change may occur, we place them on scholars' radar early in the research process so that they can inform choices about how to frame a research question, and how to approach the study of different empirical phenomena. Moreover, by treating both norms and practice as analytically productive focal points of analysis, our approach places them on an equal ontological footing and provides value for scholars as they conceive of where and what to inquire after. One goal of this approach is to minimize conceptual and methodological entrapment. A researcher who assumes norm contestation is the main pathway by which social change occurs is likely to apply that lens widely, even in situations where that may not be the most suitable strategy for making sense of what is occurring empirically. Similarly, if one assumes that practices are inherently normative – that is, practices and normativity are permanently entangled by definition – this makes it difficult to perceive situations where norms and practices may be evolving in different directions, or through different processes. In short, the approach we advance below has implications for methods and research design in addition to theoretical implications.

Plan of the Element

The remainder of this Element proceeds as follows. In Section 2, we survey a series of explicit and implicit debates within norm- and practice-oriented accounts of social change. Drawing on canonical and emerging accounts of norms, socialization, and implementation dynamics alongside varied approaches to international practice, we uncover four major debates on social change in global politics: on how to observe change, whether norms are things or processes, the role of agency, and the conditions that make change possible. Rather than attempting to directly reconcile each debate, we use this systematic survey to map existing accounts of social change to provide the theoretical scaffolding of our own analytical approach. We then develop that approach more fully in Section 3. There, we outline four analytical scenarios of change, each highlighting variable interactions between norms and practice. These scenarios should be understood as a heuristic for thinking about the relationship between norms and practices, how that relationship can vary, and how different iterations of that relationship are conducive to relative continuity or relative change. In Section 4, we demonstrate the plausibility and utility of our analytical scenarios through two brief illustrations. These empirical illustrations centre on the changing practice of two global governance norms – the norm of consular assistance for citizens abroad as applied during the COVID-19 pandemic, and on the evolving disjuncture over fifty years of the "global partnership for development" norm and practices of development, especially the rise of "partnerships" and multi-stakeholderism as means of implementing global development goals. In Section 5, we conclude by reflecting on the Element's main contributions, including our analytical scenarios, and by offering avenues for future research on social change and the interaction of norms and practices.

2 Debating Change

A rich and growing literature attempts to account for the sources of social change and the means by which stability and continuity unfold in global politics. Recent work on social change centres especially on the dynamics of norms and practice. We observe four core interrelated debates within this literature and within the growing accounts that place norms and practice in dialogue: how we can observe change in the social world; whether norms are things or dynamic processes; the role of agency and structure in social change; and the conditions under which change might occur. Our purpose in this section is not to take sides in these debates. Rather, we seek to critically and productively explore how IR scholars variably understand and account for social change. In doing so, we derive the conceptual scaffolding for the four analytical scenarios of social change that we develop and demonstrate in subsequent sections.

How to Observe Change

Perhaps the most fundamental scholarly debate on social change concerns how we observe it. Even undeniably important "changes" in global politics, such as the collapse of the Soviet Union and the end of the Cold War, are a challenge to delineate and the means of observing their effects and significance are debated (see Schindler and Willes 2015). Most norms scholarship, particularly that which recognizes norms as discrete social things, conceptualizes change in global politics by identifying a norm and corresponding rhetorical and behavioural patterns and analyzing how a norm is adopted, interpreted, enacted, and contested. Change is observable through tracing evidence of such a path. Explorations of both a norm "life cycle" and norm "localization" exemplify this trend (Finnemore and Sikkink 1998; Acharya 2004). In this view, norms leave behavioural traces, often being stated or written down (in treaties or "soft" law, statements of leaders and/or civil society, and so on), or at least their propositional content can be stated or written down. Thus, we can see that change has occurred by examining new or altered expressions of appropriate conduct for different groups. Other traditional social constructivists theorize the possibility of change through altered notions of interests and identity. The wide literature on socialization dynamics points to varied mechanisms by which actors are induced to new modes of behaviour and interests through interaction within institutions, like those of the European Union and various international organizations (e.g., Checkel 1998; Johnston 2001; Checkel 2005; Zürn and Checkel 2005), or with the liberal international order more broadly (e.g., Lake, Martin, and Risse 2021), although, of course, socialization is rarely automatic, and may be two-way, contested, resisted, or ignored (e.g., Pu 2012; He and Feng 2015; Kobayashi, Krause, and Yuan 2022; Pedersen-Macnab and Bernstein 2024). Indeed, a key argument in norms-oriented research is that international norms are often localized into particular socio-cultural contexts, especially within and by formal institutions, like international and regional organizations (Acharya 2004), and several recent interventions question its unidirectionality. Other norms-oriented researchers, as Orchard and Wiener (2024) survey, highlight the role of domestic institutions in such dynamics, shaping, forestalling, or precluding the adoption of international norms (see also Busby 2007; Simmons 2009). In addition, an expansive literature highlights not only how institutional contexts affect the norms of states and their agents, but also how varied mechanisms of social interaction within varied institutional settings shape the identity of states and their agents (Wendt 1992). In many accounts, change – be it adopting, contesting or adapting norms, or fostering novel elements of identity – is discerned by observing what analysts understand to be updated or new patterns of action, stated or assumed preferences, and declared or intuited interests gleaned from behaviour, rhetoric, or shifting justifications for action and (non)compliance with existing norms.

Practice theorists and pragmatists draw attention to similar dynamics of interactions and the possibility of change in preferences, interests, and identity. However, they pay particular attention to the impermanence of the social world rather than its normative or material structures, and they highlight the ever-present potential for change within, and unfixity of, social relations. In this view, change is a continual condition of the social world and "[s]tability ... is an illusion created by the recursive nature of practice" (Adler and Pouliot 2011, 18; see also Glas et al. 2018, 343). Moreover, practice theorists of all stripes draw analytical attention to varied levels of this social world, often highlighting the potentially mundane, quotidian interactions of life, and professional interaction as salient sites for dynamics of change and contestation. As one example, Nair (2020) demonstrates how the sociable practice of the playing of golf created a crucial "backstage" for regional diplomacy, wherein the male elite of ASEAN could diffuse conflict and through which a salient ASEAN group identity could be fostered and maintained (see also Nair 2019). To observe change – in identity, interest, or behaviour – practice-oriented accounts tend to stress the importance of examining both the thinking and behaviour of groups of actors, seeking evidence of modifications regardless of the formal rhetorical or codified markers of norm adoption. Changes in thinking and behaviour are understood as caused by subtle dynamics of learning through doing over time (Pouliot 2008). In most practice-oriented accounts of global governance, particularly diplomatic interactions, theorists draw on Pierre Bourdieu (Adler-Nissen 2011). Central to many such applications is Bourdieu's concept of *habitus*: practical and generalized dispositions and understandings of the world and one's place therein that lead to patterned interactions over time given one's position in some field or community (see Schatzki 2001; see also Standfield 2020). Many accounts centre on the habitus of groups within institutional settings, including government ministries (Loh 2020, 2024) and transnational diplomatic sites (Pouliot 2010) wherein new ways of knowing and doing are socialized and old ones replaced in rather unthinking ways. Although the recurrence of patterns, given the particularities of habitus within contexts, features prominently in such accounts, habitus can and does change (see Jackson 2009). Accounts of diplomacy, for example, highlight how diplomatic practice and habitus have changed over time, shifting from the near-exclusive preview of "gentlemanly diplomacy" of states and official representatives to include new actors and new sites (Sending, Pouliot, and Neumann 2011), including in recent years the digital realm (Hedling and Bremberg 2021; Eggeling and Adler-Nissen 2021). Thus, the skills and knowledge of competent diplomacy have shifted markedly over time.

Methodologically, accounts of practice that explicate changes in habitus and practices of diplomacy and beyond tend to adopt some form of process tracing, unearthing evidence of causal mechanisms and processes across a sequence of events which exhibit modified thinking and behaviour (Bennett and Checkel 2014). Pouliot's "practice tracing," for example, centres on the recognition of localized and contingent causality and seeks to "develop or fine-tune" accounts of causal mechanisms of change in practice over time (2014, 237; 2020, 240). Similarly, for Pratt, this process involves "tracing transactions," with a particular focus on the co-constitution of actors and agency such that some actors are able to reposition themselves as outside the categorical bounds of normative action (2020, 17). These approaches are well-suited to tracing subtle changes in habitus, including the understanding and enactment of norms and practice over time, which may or may not be formally institutionalized. However, as Hopf (2018, 689) notes, practice theory's appraisal of change tends to centre on endogenous, ubiquitous, and often minimal changes, and not "the kind of meaningful and significant change that we mostly care about in the study of world politics." Thus, debate remains over what types of change count as "meaningful" and how best to observe and account for them.

A second, and related, level of debate on this point centres on questions of data. Speaking in broad strokes, traditional norm-centred research often observes the adoption or institutionalization of norms through an interrogation of official statements and documents. Acharya (2014), for example, uncovers the socio-cultural and political-legal norms of ASEAN regionalism largely through a detailed survey of the organization's documentary sources and official statements from leaders. Whereas attention to discursive representations is productive to explore the normative terrain of institutional contexts (see also Glas 2022, 67–68), practice theorists interrogate what is done by practitioners therein, that is, why and how those practitioners navigate that terrain – normative, material, and otherwise. Substantively, however, practice theorists have long focused on questions of international diplomacy, an area of inquiry whose contexts are often challenging to access and observe, to say nothing of conducting immersive ethnographic inquiry. As a result, a trend among practice-focused studies is to rely on varied forms of qualitative interviewing, speaking with practitioners about their – and others' – experiences and perspectives (e.g., Pouliot 2010; Adler-Nissen 2014a; Glas 2022; Laurence 2024b). A common logic for this choice of research design is to "(imperfectly) make up for the impossibility of participant observation" (Pouliot 2010, 70). In exploring continuity in regional conflict management practices, for example, Glas examined how practitioners understood and responded to crises by asking questions that prompted reflection on what officials did and did not do, and why, in order to "generate lines to read between and to offer means of arriving at imperfect understandings of thought and practice" (Glas 2022, 68). This common approach to uncovering elements of practice, however, is increasingly questioned. Nair (2020), for example, has suggested that practice theorists need to broaden their investigations, shifting from a default towards interviewing to embracing a "hanging out" approach, adapting the lessons of an "ethnographic sensibility" (Schatz 2009) for contexts wherein direct observation is not possible. In Nair's view, prolonged interaction with participants – beyond formal participant observation – can make possible ethnographic insights and data into thinking and practice (2020, 3). Hopf has more directly critiqued the viability of interviewing to uncover the "taken-for-granted doxa of diplomatic practitioners" that Pouliot and others seek to explore (2011, 773). Yet Hopf, himself, makes a sound case for thinking about the dynamics of practice and the situated background knowledge that makes it possible through his own inductive, thick narrative analysis of identity and meaning-making. His approach to exploring the role of self-identity for Soviet and Russian foreign policy through discourse analysis – drawing on a range of sources, from official documents to popular fiction – is grounded in a deep commitment to contextualization and intertextualization that aligns with a broadly ethnographic sensibility (2002, 26; see also Glas 2022, 78–80). Similarly, in his account of praxiography – the "practice of doing practice theory driven research" – Bueger (2014, 385) highlights the importance of document analysis, which he identifies as a valuable strategy for gathering knowledge about practice, both in conjunction with other methods and on its own (see also Bueger 2023). Indeed, he describes documents as one type of artefact into which practices can be inscribed; documents provide "access points" for deciphering practice because they are a core material in policymaking, one of the main artefacts in international negotiations, and part of the "basic material out of which the field of political practice is made" (2014, 398). While not universally embraced, praxiographic document analyses allow for the study of practices *around* documents, including how they are written and embedded in wider practices and use (Bueger 2023, 151).

We see this ongoing debate around how one can understand and observe norms and practice as both unsettled and as productive for richer empirical work across the norms- and practice-based orientations. We remain sympathetic to the utility of interpretive-oriented interviewing and discourse analysis as viable means of exploring dynamics of norms and practice, particularly when developed in tandem with other elements of research – observation, hanging out, ethnographic immersion[3] – that may augment or extend the ability to experience and observe how practitioners make sense of and interact with their social worlds.

Norms as Things and Processes

A second division centres on how to understand norms and their relationship to practice. This debate captures differences between accounts of norms as social things, processes, normative configurations, normative inventories, or norms as the stuff of practices.

Early norm scholarship presented norms as relatively static social "things": standards of appropriate conduct whose existence, diffusion, and effects are also assumed to be relatively static (Katzenstein 1996; Krook and True 2010, 106). This work treated norms as modular and able to be adopted and institutionalized "as is" by states or organizations (Finnemore and Sikkink 1998). These accounts paid little attention to the potential for contestation over the meaning of norms or variation in their performance across contexts and over time. This characterization is not surprising, given this scholarship's impulse to demonstrate normativity in global politics itself (e.g., Finnemore 1996; Keck and Sikkink 1998). In this view, social change occurs as discrete norms are adopted, institutionalized, or internalized and come to shape behaviour in new and observable ways.

However, an array of more recent scholarship is critical of the assumption of norms as static things and views norms as inherently contested and dynamic social processes (Wiener 2004; Epstein 2008; Krook and True 2010; Orchard and Wiener 2024). Contestation is inherently relational – it can only be understood in relation to other norms or structures. In this view, the meaning of norms and their enactment in practice across contexts and over time is essentially unsettled and variable. Norms may be localized to align with existing "cognitive priors" or erode and evolve in accordance with deeply held assumptions about competing "normative priors" (Acharya 2004, 251; Coe 2019, 19). In Wiener's prominent account, norms derive "meaning-in-use" (2009, True and Wiener

---

[3] Another promising methodological innovation – as yet not explicitly used by IR practice-focused scholars – is team-based "collaborative event ethnography," where groups of researchers use a common analytical framework to treat negotiations or events as "field sites." It allows attendance at potentially hundreds of official and unofficial meetings during single large-scale events like multilateral negotiations to track how a plurality of participants pursue interests, interact, practice diplomacy, and articulate ideas. The method arguably can better make visible plural practices and discourses and how they interact in a field. However, it is resource intensive and, like other ethnographic approaches, is limited to sites with access. See Brosius and Campell (2010) and Marion Suiseeya and Zanotti (2019).

2019). Change occurs and is observable as norms are enacted in variable ways with variable effects, dependent on contextual and local social dynamics. Pratt (2020) moves further in the direction of understanding norms only through their practice with his pragmatist and relational account of the "multi-dimensionality and interactivity" of norms. Such "normative configurations," as he terms them, are understood and observed as "arrangements of ongoing, interacting practices establishing action-specific regulation, value orientation, and avenues of contestation" (2020, 12). Similarly, Lesch and Loh (2022, 3) argue that "taking practices as something that shapes norms, or practices as an effect of norms," is at odds with a relational approach to international practices; instead, they describe normativity as "an ongoing achievement *in and through* practice."

Finally, a few practice scholars have derived lessons from norm contestation and localization literatures and, as a result, similarly begin their analyses with a conceptualization of norms as variable processes that derive meaning through use. However, these scholars tend to see norms as referents for practical action and practices reflective of normativity within particular CoPs or different fields (e.g., Bode and Karlsrud 2019). The unreflexive qualities of established practices shape how actors pursue the action prescribed by norms. In the case of the norm of "people-oriented governance," for example, Glas and Balogun (2020) find that different actors understand and enact the same norm in divergent ways because of established logics of practicality, leading to different changes in governance in the ASEAN and the Economic Community of West African States. Meanwhile, Lesch and Loh (2022, 3–5) suggest that practices related to China's Belt and Road Initiative (BRI) are enacted in international spaces that are shaped by multiple overlapping fields with competing "normative inventories" that provide different standards for evaluating, and potentially contesting, BRI practices.

This debate has an ontological character that we find largely unresolvable, but also extremely limiting for theory development. Thus, as we elaborate in Section 3, instead of seeking a resolution, we make an explicit move to place norms and practices on equal ontological footing, refusing to reduce one to the other. This move allows us to model variation in the relationship between norms and practices that produce different patterns of change and continuity, our analytic goal. Such a move may not satisfy purists in either camp. However, in practice many scholars treat them as separate when they move from abstract conceptualizations to theory development around their relationships to institutions, governance, and change, as we highlighted in Section 1. Moreover, even the strongest defenders of relational ontologies in social theory recognize that such analytic moves may be necessary for theory construction (Emirbayer 1997).

Agency

A third division concerns variable accounts of reflection and agency in change. While much of the literature suggests a dichotomy – change derives either from agentic, deliberative, and reflection-driven action *or* through unreflexive processes and behaviours – a spectrum of positions is visible across both norm and practice-based accounts (see Hopf 2018). On one end of this spectrum, traditional norms research tends to assume that actors consciously diffuse and socialize norms. Normative considerations shape the calculus of rational actors, from entrepreneurial non-governmental actors to organizational officials, and lead to changes in behaviour. In this "pyramid" account of change, purposive, deliberative reflection drives social change and produces something "new" through strategic action (Pouliot 2020, 5; see also Czarniawska 2009).

Practice theorists, on the other end of this spectrum, stress the logic of practicality. They highlight the role of tacit knowledge and practical agency in change, understanding and explaining "change in practice through practice" (Hopf 2018, 692). Practice theorists attest that most of what individuals do, they do as a matter of course and without active reflection or appraisal of expected outcomes (Adler and Pouliot 2011). Background or practical knowledge, the "stock of inarticulate know-how learned in and through practice," delimits freedom of action (Pouliot 2010, 28). In this account, agency is shaped less by the push of interests (and conditioned by relational dynamics) than it is pulled or "elicited by the web of practices" within which social action takes place (Pouliot 2020, 2). This position does not mean individuals are uncreative or unthinking. Rather, individuals rely on "regulated improvisation" (Bourdieu 1977, 11; Cornut 2018) and deploy creative, artful, but "unarticulated strategies without conscious strategizing or reflection," while the inherent "wiggle room" in the enactment of practices drives change over time (Adler and Pouliot 2011, 7; Cornut 2018; Hopf 2018, 692; Rösch 2020). Thus, change unfolds akin to the construction of an "anthill" – messily and through micro-level and unreflexive movements to produce something "new" over time (Pouliot 2020, 5). These accounts often present "practical agency" as fundamentally distinct or "ontologically prior" to rationality and "reflexive agency" in reference to the logics of consequence, appropriateness, or arguing (Pouliot 2010; Cornut 2018; Hopf 2018). Pouliot's (2020, 7) "pulling theory" of agency, for example, highlights not the "intentional agency" inherent in historical institutionalist and rational choice accounts of change, but the play of practice in shaping the bounds of possible action.

Between the two ends of the spectrum, several scholars offer accounts of both reflection and unreflexive agency affecting change. In a forceful critique of practice theory's focus on practical agency, Hopf underscores that "conscious reflection still matters" (2018, 689). Laurence (2024a, 1, 2024b) develops this line of argument by analyzing individual agency within UN peace operations, showing that "reflective agency" and "practical agency" both contribute to changes in peacekeeping practice, and she examines the social, political, and institutional conditions that are conducive to change through conscious reflection. However, the conditions under which one matters more than the other are still debated, as we explore below.

Before doing so, we pause to explicate related disagreements over the role of power and influence in social change. Practice accounts underscore that change may occur because actors' behaviour signals some (new) normal in and through doing (Pouliot 2008, 283). Neumann suggests that when authoritative actors "act as if" something is normal or natural, it may become so. For example, Norwegian officials were able to "narrate into existence" peaceful regional relations with Russia at the end of the Cold War by demonstrating that "relations between Norway and Russia had 'always' been friendly at the grassroots level – except for the last 70 years of communism" (Neumann 2002, 640–641).

Thus, while power may manifest in varied ways in all instances of change, particular actors may have the ability to effect change more than others. In practice-oriented accounts, this ability is understood as contextually bound and relational. Certain diplomatic officials, for example, may be "virtuosos" with a "practical mastery" of their craft within particular contexts and thus able to affect change (Adler-Nissen 2016; Pouliot 2016; Cornut 2018). In these accounts, this kind of "emergent power" is contingent, contested, and relational. For example, the "penholding" power available to certain actors in the UN Security Council (UNSC) represents an "evident competence" that allows for influence (Adler-Nissen and Pouliot 2014). Institutional context may also affect opportunities for agency. For example, Pouliot (2020) identifies "grey areas" in many institutional arrangements – semi-formal areas where practices may be "self-monitored" as opposed to areas dictated by formal rules or informal realms where custom and the "anthill" model prevail. In examining changes in practices in the UNSC, Pouliot (2020, 17) finds that this grey area of semi-formality provides opportunities for the Presidency, for example, to set the agenda and engage in power struggles over its practices.

Conditions for Change

A final debate within norm and practice literatures concerns the conditions under which social change is likely to occur. Disagreements centre on when and how actors turn to reflexive action, the variable effects of institutional structures and density, and the role of exogenous dynamics at moments of critical junctures. While practice theorists draw attention to the role of practical agency and norm theorists tend to highlight the role of deliberative and conscious reflection, an increasingly broad group of scholars attempts to reconcile both, examining the conditions under which reflection is likely or not and how contexts interact with ways of thinking. Cornut (2018, 713), for example, recognizes, "What international practitioners do is both contingent on the situations they face and path-dependent." Laurence (2024b) articulates a similar interrelationship between processes of deliberative "innovation" and practical, unreflexive "improvisation" to explain practice change in UN peace operations. Similarly, Pouliot (2020, 3) suggests that under certain conditions, actors "do not contradict their interests but simply act on them in contextually enabled ways." The balance between reflection and practical agency and the conditions under which one is more likely to drive change is less clear and often captured only in broad heuristic terms, such as the "grey zone" institutional space referenced above. In account of unreflexive change and the building of "anthills," as Hopf (2018, 694) notes, "There are no scope conditions for practical agency as we are constantly executing practices, and in so doing, changing them, if only marginally." However, Hopf articulates several important scope conditions under which reflexive change is likely.

In Hopf's (2018) view, profound change is more likely at times of surprise when shocks interrupt some sense of "normal." This may include confronting and recognizing "meaningful and effective" differences or facing "extreme" problems and exogenous crises (Hopf 2018, 696, 701). There is widespread recognition across literatures that major exogenous developments may prompt reflection on otherwise institutionalized, internalized, or unreflexively-practiced behaviours and norms. Historical institutionalist scholarship, for example, has long held that crises present conditions under which social change is likely to occur (e.g., Thelen and Steinmo 1992; Pierson 2000; Zürn 2016). Similarly, some practice scholarship highlights the role of crises and disjunctures in change. Radical, exogenous shocks may upend established ways of knowing and doing leading to the potential for important social change – including the end of practices as certain actors respond to these shocks (Stein 2011). These actors include those less socialized into normative or practical communities and those at the margins or liminal spaces of a community or field (Hopf 2018, 696; see also Glas and Martel 2024).

A major takeaway from this survey of existing debates around social change is that change and stability unfold through myriad paths. Moreover, the acknowledgement that "shocks" or "crisis" are often precursors to change highlights a growing recognition among many IR scholars of the necessity of a relational ontology to confront uncertainty in the real world of global politics, where many contemporary problems reflect an acceleration of forces that increase contingency, complexity, unknown unknowns, and historical developments that cannot be anticipated, from technological innovation like AI to polycrises (Burrows and Gnad 2018; Katzenstein 2022; Flockhart 2022; Lawrence et al. 2024; Bernstein 2024). Uncertainty, in turn, can reconfigure political landscapes or the "background" within which social change takes place. In part for these reasons, we do not propose a theory of change as such. Rather, we identify processes of change in relation to this background in which norms and practices are enmeshed. Our framework thus recognizes that relative change and continuity in social relations may be the product of a *lack* of reflection by largely unreflexive agents who uphold ways of doing over long periods or alter behaviours through the play of practice over time. Change and continuity may be influenced by varied structural conditions and background relations that stymie or promote critical reflection leading to the emergence of novel ideas and modes of interaction or precluding them. Alternatively, both change and stability may be produced through active and purposive actions *and* through rather inadvertent behaviours, variably shaped by powerful social agents with intentions to affect change and stability or not. In short, the literature on norms and practice demonstrates that the means by which change and stability unfold in global politics are many.

Rather than treating these insights as debates to be adjudicated, we see them as conceptual foundations for a set of analytical scenarios that capture varieties of norm and practice change. Indeed, our goal in this Element is to systematically describe a range of pathways by which social change can occur. To date, these pathways have typically been examined separately, or sometimes sequentially, an approach that can inadvertently limit the range of possibilities to which scholars are attuned. Thoroughly describing a wider range of scenarios is useful because it primes scholars to recognize modes and types of change early in the research process, including scenarios that they might otherwise have ignored. Importantly, our scenarios can be leveraged in both deductive analysis – as a starting point for thinking about how social change can occur in global politics – and in inductive analysis, as tools for making theoretical sense of empirical phenomena that initially seem puzzling. Our framework has the added benefit of synthesizing insights from recent debates in the literature on both norms and international practices. In doing so, it demonstrates the analytical payoff of an agnostic approach – one that takes relational critiques of the norms literature seriously without jettisoning the concept of norms altogether, and one that centres the concept of practice without restricting attention to practices of norm implementation or norm contestation (cf. Orchard and Wiener 2024, 14).

In short, we intend these scenarios as a novel analytical framework that can help scholars approach research questions and empirical puzzles in new ways. We develop and define each in the following section.

3 Four Analytical Scenarios of Social Change

The previous section critically surveyed scholarship on social change and continuity by drawing on accounts of norms and practice and, increasingly, by placing them in productive dialogue. As we showed, within this rich literature there are four core debates concerning how to observe change, whether norms are things or processes, the role of agency, and the conditions for meaningful change. The vibrancy of these debates underscores the varied means by which social change occurs in global politics, and it illustrates the importance of being attentive, both theoretically and methodologically, to the multiple pathways by which change can happen. In this section, we draw on these debates to offer four analytical scenarios that capture varieties of norm and practice change in an attempt to catalogue the varied ways through which social change occurs. Our articulation of these varied pathways to relative change or continuity does not in itself unearth strictly novel dynamics that the rich – and growing – literature surveyed has not suggested. Rather, our framework places disparate and often siloed accounts of norms and practices, and accounts that attempt to bridge these concepts, into productive dialogue and develops a systematic articulation of the pathways through which the varied relationships between norms and practices affect change and continuity. Our four analytical scenarios are as follows: a tight coupling of norms and practices; inadvertent errors in practice; unacknowledged disjunctures between norms and practices; and deliberate acts of resistance or transgression. Each scenario should be understood as a lens for thinking about the relationship between norms and practices, how this relationship can vary, and how different iterations of that relationship are conducive to relative continuity or relative social change. We explore each scenario in turn, providing a definitional discussion, exploring relevant accounts of change and continuity that speak to the dynamics of each, and highlighting how each scenario speaks to the previously examined conceptual debates. Within each scenario, we identify how norms and practices are understood, the role of agency and reflection, the structural conditions that make change possible, and how one may observe social change and its quality and importance.

As we foreshadowed above, our scenarios necessarily rest on an explicit ontological move. In contrast to the earlier sharp divisions in the scholarship that made either norms or practices their primary "unit of analysis," we place them on equal ontological footing. This allows us to examine new questions about the relationship between them and how changes in one affect changes in the other (Bourbeau 2017, 171). Rather than assume that practice change equates with norm implementation, or that all practices are inherently normative, our move opens up space to explore variation in the relationship between normativity and practice, with important implications for patterns of continuity and change.

To avoid misunderstanding, we do not dismiss the notion that norms and practices are mutually constitutive and that there is a constant interplay between them. Indeed, norms – or normativity, as some scholars conceptualize it – acquire meaning in and *through* practice (Wiener 2009, 176; Lesch and Loh 2022, 3). Similarly, if practices are understood to be "competent performances," then standards for judging competence often have a strong normative dimension (Adler and Pouliot 2011, 7; see also Gadinger 2022). Nonetheless, as has long been acknowledged by even the strongest proponents of a relational ontology, an extreme adherence to this position inevitably creates a "problem of *boundary specification*, of moving from flows of transactions to clearly demarcated units of study, from continuity to discontinuity" (emphasis in original, Emirbayer 1997, 303). We do not dismiss these important linkages, nor do we deny their processual, relational character. However, we see the distinction between norms and practices as more than simply heuristic, but as a necessary ontological move that provides analytical leverage and enables methodologies to support that analysis to improve understandings of social change. Examining norms and practices separately, and often in interaction, makes it possible to examine changes in the relationship between them (Archer 1988, 258–259; Carlsnaes 1992; Bouris and Fernández-Molina 2024).

Following this approach, our scenarios capture variations in the relationship between norms and practices to show different modes of social change. These scenarios are not meant to be exhaustive or mutually exclusive. They are analytical lenses – or even ideal types – that allow us to identify, think through, and compare different pathways by which social change might occur. The benefits of doing so are both theoretical and methodological. Theoretically, our move overcomes the tendency to examine these pathways separately, which can create biases or blind spots in where or how we see or expect change. Describing a wider range of scenarios is useful because it prepares scholars to recognize different modes and types of change early in the research process, including scenarios that they might otherwise have missed.

Our ontological move also informs our methodology. In each scenario, we both trace how norms and practices develop and change independently and examine their interaction over time, looking for whether they reinforce or create tension in institutional arrangements. We remain analytically open to varied ways they may be interrelated. This approach moves us beyond several scholars who, on the one hand, collapse norms and practice (e.g., Pratt 2020, and many other practice theorists) or who, on the other hand, foreground either norm compliance (e.g., Chayes and Chayes 1993, Finnemore 1996, and many early norm scholars) or, alternatively, norm contestation, tension, and hypocrisy (e.g., Bouris and Fernández-Molina 2024, and many others centred on contestation). As we foreshadowed earlier, our framework avoids truncating processes of change in ways that are driven by ontological choices and ensuing areas of analytic focus. This has methodological benefits in addition to theoretical ones insofar as it attunes scholars to a wider range of analytical possibilities early in the research process, allowing them to adjust their research questions and research design accordingly.

Scenario 1: Tight Coupling

Much of the literature on norms and practices focuses on situations where the two are tightly coupled. Consequently, practices are often equated with internalized norms, or normativity is taken to be an inherent dimension of practice. In these cases, there is a positive feedback loop in which shared beliefs about "what constitutes competence reinforce and reproduce existing understandings of what a norm means and what it requires" (Bernstein and Laurence 2022, 85). In other words, there is a substantial overlap between standards for judging competence and shared beliefs about appropriate behaviour. Many norm scholars frame changes in practice in terms of compliance with, or implementation of, relatively static norms that purposive agents can either promote or resist. In this view, compliance describes adherence to an existing norm, while norm implementation is the process by which actors bring their practices into alignment with a new norm (Betts and Orchard 2014, 6–7). This type of research builds on early constructivist work, which sought to demonstrate the impact of ideational factors like norms, culture, and identity and persuade skeptics – especially those from rationalist and materialist research traditions – that norms influence behaviour (Finnemore and Sikkink 2001, 393). Early proponents of social constructivism in IR were, therefore, deeply invested in showing that norms – usually studied as "single entities" – had direct, tangible effects on practice, and that changes in the former yield changes in the latter (Percy and Sandholtz 2022, 945). For example, Katzenstein (1996, 5, 25–26) argued that social factors like norms, identity, and culture shape states' perception of their own interests, and that this has meaningful effects on their national security policies and the behaviours that flow from those policies. Finnemore (2003, 52–53) examines shifting patterns of military intervention, arguing that they are linked to changes in states' shared understandings of what constitutes legitimate cause for military action. This focus on how practices change alongside norms is understandable. Making a strong case for "tight coupling" was a critical move for the social constructivist research program because it posed a clear challenge to those who doubted the "real world" impact of intersubjective knowledge.

Critics point out that these early efforts were limited by linear assumptions about norm implementation – by the idea that norms were modular things that could emerge, become institutionalized, and then alter practices in specific ways. However, as scholars who attest to the processual qualities of norms recognize, change is not unidirectional nor are the contours of change predetermined when a norm is adopted or institutionalized (Krook and True 2010). Norms themselves can emerge or be gradually transformed through practice, particularly given the "wiggle room" of all practices, however competently enacted (Adler and Pouliot 2011, 7). Similarly, as we have explored above, practice theorists find that practices constitute and reproduce social structures. However, reproduction must not be equated with stasis. Practices are dynamic and continuously evolving; stability is a perception that emerges out of incremental adjustments that practitioners make to suit their environment (Doty 1997, 16; Adler and Pouliot 2011, 16). Thus, "tight coupling" should not be viewed as the opposite of change. This scenario is meant to capture situations where there is significant overlap between standards for judging competence and shared beliefs about appropriateness, with the understanding that neither is ever completely static and change is always possible. In this respect, the scenario extends relational critiques of early constructivist scholarship, which treated norms as static things and assumed that practices could be easily classified as either "compliant" or "non-compliant." Instead, it provides a conceptual framework for thinking about the mutual entanglement of norms and practices, and how it can obscure patterns of institutional change. We might expect such a scenario to unfold in highly institutionalized contexts, with limited exogenous pressure to reflect on "how things are done." However, while change is possible in such situations, it is likely to unfold as the endogenous and ubiquitous change that Hopf (2018) finds of less significance for the social world.

Scenario 2: Change through "Incompetence"

In the second scenario, practices are performed incorrectly, or "incompetently," usually by accident or through misunderstanding. This is especially common in settings where resource constraints or a lack of expertise prevent an actor from competently enacting a norm. Over the short term, this type of accidental incompetence is perceived as such by members of a community or field of interaction. This scenario may occur in heavily institutionalized settings or in looser social settings. Regardless of context, inadvertently incompetent practice does not immediately undermine the bond between practice and a broader normative commitment (Adler-Nissen and Pouliot 2014). Depending on the setting, it could spark complaints from others or lead to a loss of status for the incompetent performer within a community or group. These correctives might allow incompetent performers to recognize the error and "do better" in the future, which may serve to reinforce established expectations or ways of doing things within a community. Alternatively, such inadvertently incompetent performances might be overlooked, dismissed as insignificant, or forgotten, with little immediate impact on broader norms. Over the long term, however, ongoing or persistently incompetent performances may erode or transform the sense of oughtness that flows from a norm, thereby weakening the link between practice and formal articulations of a given norm (Panke and Petersohn 2012). This scenario has elements in common with Oksamytna and Wilén's (2022, 2367) concept of incidental norm adaptation, which – unlike strategic adaptation or principled adaptation – is "a result of unanticipated factors or events." This dynamic underscores the role of chance when it comes to accounting for change in global politics. As Oksamytna and Wilén (2022) demonstrate, meaningful change may result from unintentional alterations of behaviour.

The likelihood of seeing norm erosion or broader and meaningful social change as a result of accidental incompetence depends on a variety of factors. These include the strength of a norm, its degree of precision, its relationship with other cross-cutting norms and practices, levels of permissiveness within a community, and an actor's position within a given community. A newcomer within a community, for instance, might be forgiven for accidental incompetence while a longstanding member may be expected to know and act better (Lave and Wenger 1991, 101). The response from members of a group or community, then, may vary and thus the effects of the inadvertent divergence may vary. Moreover, norms "derive durability from their embeddedness in larger normative structures," like legal systems (Percy and Sandholtz 2022, 946). This interconnectedness underlines the fact that norms are just one "component" of institutions, and higher degrees of embeddedness may also affect prospects for recognizing or punishing incompetent practices. In terms of long-term impact, power and authority are also important factors. Historically influential actors within a community are more likely to create precedents through their behaviour, even if unintentionally. Authoritative actors behaving *as if* something is normal, natural, or congruent with established norms may have the effect of manifesting these ways of knowing or doing as such (see

Neumann 2009; Glas 2022). Moreover, the likelihood that inadvertent incompetence will remain genuinely accidental for long enough to erode actors' sense of obligation to a norm will depend on context and the extent to which accidental incompetence is punished as opposed to overlooked.

When it passes largely unremarked, an actor may not realize their mistake and may persist with similar practices, creating the possibility for change through accidental incompetence. Indeed, Florini (1996, 372), in an early piece on normative evolution in IR, noted that international norms are susceptible to misunderstandings, and that "copying errors" in norm implementation can become a source of variation and change. However, when incompetence provokes negative reactions from others, it becomes much harder to claim that similar transgressions are unintentional. These two possibilities speak to the debate about when – and whether – changes in practices involve conscious reflection and contestation. They also raise a thornier question about how to distinguish accidental incompetence from deliberate transgressions. Admittedly, distinguishing accidental incompetence from deliberate acts can be challenging. For example, almost 200 states formally accepted the reporting obligations outlined in the 2005 International Health Regulations (IHR), but the COVID-19 pandemic revealed that many governments lacked the capacity to gather and analyze the data required to meet those obligations in practice (WHO 2005, 1; Katz and Fischer 2010: 4; Mallapaty 2022). There are political, institutional, and practical reasons for this, including normative contestation that leads states to deliberately evade reporting requirements (Hathaway and Philips-Robins 2020). It is important to recognize, however, that resource constraints, the need for specialized expertise, and myriad other challenges associated with data collection during the COVID-19 pandemic, also made it challenging for many states to provide timely, accurate, and detailed information as required under the IHR (Lloyd-Sherlock et al. 2021). In short, incompetent practice can be unintentional.

From an analytical perspective, however, it is difficult for observers to gauge an actor's underlying intentions. As any parent knows, claiming to have transgressed by accident – rather than on purpose – is often a first line of defence when an actor faces criticism for that transgression. However skeptical we might be of such claims, we know that accidents can and do occur. Even if intentions are hard to glean, we believe a useful distinction can be made between overt contestation, of both the thin and thick varieties, and accidental incompetence. That said, the extent to which inadvertent incompetence drives meaningful change is very much an open question. A review of the secondary literature suggests that it is both possible and plausible, even if it is the exception. At the very least, however, we should allow for the possibility that change can occur through inadvertent incompetence and look for creative ways to probe its impact empirically. It is in this spirit of theoretical and methodological openness that we include the scenario here, even though we do not fully develop it in Section 4. As we note in Section 5, this is likely to be a fruitful area for future research.

Scenario 3: Disjunctures and Change

Our third scenario has received less attention in the scholarly literature. It describes the following situation: when standards for judging competence and shared beliefs about appropriateness gradually drift apart, but not through errors or deliberate contestation. Rather, drift occurs through micro changes or alterations in existing practices, which occur as part of the ongoing "play" of practice (Bueger and Gadinger 2015, 449) or, alternatively, normative change previously "entangled" with mutually reinforcing practice change instead occurs while practices remain unaltered (Bouris and Fernández-Molina 2024). Evolving practices may still be interpreted as consistent with established norms, more or less consistent with what Ruggie (1982) characterized as "norm-governed" change; these are likely to be situations where observers perceive a change while many practitioners do not. Yet practices require ongoing reinterpretation and justification vis-à-vis those norms as they become increasingly divorced from practices previously associated with those norms. Furthermore, in this scenario, justifications are articulated in familiar terms – in ways that reinforce or stabilize established normativity despite novel ways of doing things. These justifications may be contested or found wanting by members of a community, but new patterns of action are not, themselves, perceived as incompetent vis-à-vis an established understanding of appropriateness. We understand this scenario in terms of "decoupling," although practitioners are unlikely to share this view and frequently engage in discursive attempts to "recouple" new practices with established norms.

We have observed exactly this dynamic in previous research, such as in the case of UN peace operations where novel practices like conducting joint military operations with host states to attack and suppress insurgent groups are still described as "impartial" and justified in familiar normative terms (Bernstein and Laurence 2022). While change in this scenario involves small and perhaps incremental changes in practice over time, more research is needed to determine how much tension can exist between practices and norms before social change is widely recognized. While norms may be permissive, adaptable, or even reveal "organized hypocrisy" (Krasner 1999), over time, as hypocrisy becomes more apparent and provokes political conflict (Bouris and Fernández-Molina 2024), we hypothesize that there would be a "pull toward congruence" over the long term (Bernstein and Laurence 2022).

As in our "accidental incompetence" scenario, the disjuncture scenario highlights the unintentional dimensions of practice that can lead to profound social change. Agency extends to creative adaptation within a web of cross-cutting practices, but not to a conscious strategy aimed at bringing about broader change. It also demonstrates that practitioners themselves may not be aware of how their community's practices appear to outsiders, who might identify changes that practitioners either do not detect or prefer not to articulate (Laurence 2019, 17–18). In doing so, it serves as a useful corrective to theories that equate practice change with norm implementation, or which subsume the concept of normativity within the concept of practice (Rouse 2001, 199). It underlines the value of distinguishing shared beliefs about appropriateness from shared standards for judging competence. While there may be significant overlap between these two types of intersubjective knowledge – as in our first scenario – they can also evolve in different directions over time. Finally, it raises interesting questions for future research about the conditions under which such disjunctures might arise in the first place, and the conditions under which they might subside.

Scenario 4: Change through Contestation

Our final scenario is more familiar and well-documented, especially among scholars who study norm emergence and contestation. It describes situations where "incompetent" performances are calculated acts of resistance or transgression. This scenario is similar to the concept of "behavioural contestation," developed by Stimmer and Wisken to describe contestation that occurs through action rather than words (Stimmer and Wisken 2019, 519). These actions constitute overt challenges to existing norms. They often spring from a conscious desire among actors with power resources to affect change by modifying or replacing norms, thereby re-shaping behaviour. In this sense, such actions might be best understood through a logic of "inappropriateness," as opposed to a logic of practicality (Finnemore and Sikkink 1998, 897–898). The dynamics in this scenario are highlighted by scholars of norm contestation, who emphasize complexity, fragmentation, overlap, and the disagreements that arise from "collisions" between different norms (Kreuder-Sonnen and Zürn 2020, 241). Even when these frictions are minimal, norms are not homogenous things with a single meaning. They are always "works-in-progress" that need to be interpreted, and a single norm can yield widely divergent practices (Krook and True 2010, 104). This means that – in addition to contestation about which norms should prevail in a given situation and why – contestation about what "counts" as the implementation of dominant norms is ubiquitous. Both types of contestation can drive change insofar as practices are altered to reflect normative changes, and norms evolve through debates about what they require in practice (Sandholtz 2008; Wiener 2009).

This scenario can take two forms, akin to change through "thin" or "thick" contestation (Adler-Nissen and Pouliot 2014, 895). Change may be a product of limited, reflexive contestation over what counts as the competent enactment of a norm. In one classic study about the norm against wartime plunder, Sandholtz (2008, 121) shows that disputes "inevitably reveal shifting social understandings of the rules and how they should apply in practice;" once a norm against plunder had emerged, arguments about what it required served to further clarify, elaborate, and formalize the norm. This type of thin contestation does not involve wholesale rejection of the norm in question but rather the refinement or clarification of existing rules and how they should be applied in particular situations. Serey, Bivens, and Glas (2024) demonstrate a similar dynamic in Southeast Asian multilateralism as officials from ASEAN have debated not the appropriateness of institutionalized norms of non-interference or "ASEAN centrality," but how those existent norms ought to be deployed in specific situations, such as when attempting to respond to the 2021 coup in Myanmar. The organization, as the authors show, is changing how it responds to such crises not because of direct contestation over those institutionalized norms per se, but rather through contestation over how agreed norms ought to be understood and enacted in this case. Change, however, may also be a product of efforts to erode or replace an existing norm (Panke and Petersohn 2012, 722–724). This type of thick contestation is similar to what might, in a domestic context, be understood as civil disobedience. It foregrounds the power of individuals and the role of agents as change-makers. In this respect, it has more in common with early work on norm "life cycles," especially the "norm emergence" phase, which highlights the role of norm entrepreneurs – like those campaigning in favour of women's suffrage in the early twentieth century – and their use of persuasion or civil disobedience to advance new standards for judging appropriateness (Finnemore and Sikkink 1998, 896–898). Adler-Nissen captures this dynamic and explores its potential to bring about change in her work on stigma management. States that do not conform to "normal" standards are not just passive objects of socialization; they are active agents that can deliberately embrace transgressive identities and behaviour. In some cases, they deliberately "challenge a dominant moral discourse by wearing their stigma as a badge of honor" (Adler-Nissen 2014b, 144). She presents the example of Cuba, explaining how the Cuban government has framed

American efforts to isolate the country as a source of pride and showing how this strategy has succeeded in altering public perceptions of the United States, making it seem like the transgressive state in the relationship.

Taking a broader view, we argue that the four scenarios presented in this section provide a useful framework for thinking about the relationship between norms and practices, the variation in that relationship, and how different manifestations of the relationship contribute to both change and continuity in global politics. We must also reiterate that these scenarios are intended to serve as heuristics; they do not capture the interplay between norms and practices in all its complexity. Still, they provide valuable tools for analyzing that interplay, both theoretically and empirically.

In the next section, we demonstrate these scenarios' usefulness by showing how they can be applied to improve our understanding of norms, practices, and change in global politics.

4 Applications

We developed the four analytical scenarios in the previous section to explore relative change and continuity in global politics. In this section, we draw from the field of global governance to offer two fleshed-out empirical illustrations of what our framework can offer. They demonstrate the dynamics of several of our scenarios and show how each captures important aspects of variation in modes of social change. Collectively, these two empirical examples illustrate the three different scenarios that we consider most prevalent and significant when it comes to explaining social change (scenarios 1, 3, and 4). The first example explores change and continuity in global governance norms in the face of the COVID-19 pandemic, with a focus on norms and practices related to consular support for citizens abroad (scenario 1). We then turn to the norm of a "global partnership for development," and the interplay of norms and practices over the last 55+ years, initially leading to growing disjunctures (scenario 3) and, as those disjunctures became difficult to ignore in the negotiation of the Sustainable Development Goals (SDGs), increasingly overt contestation (scenario 4). We recognize that these illustrations can only be suggestive of the full applicability of our framework, but we present them to provide some guidance on research and to illustrate their potential power to identify and understand the dynamics of social change.

In each case, we trace both norms and practices, paying particular attention to their interplay and being open to observing patterns of alignment, disjuncture, and contestation, as per our methodological discussion above. Methodologically, we follow Bueger (2014, 2023) in relying primarily on analysis of texts where norms and practices are inscribed, because in these cases they are among "the basic material out of which ... political practice is made" and norms are articulated. In addition, we mine secondary scholarly observations of norms and practices, along with some primary data on discourse and practices. Because we are interested in norm and practice dynamics over time, in one case over 55+ years, this approach is the most tractable and appropriate.

Still, we recognize that deeper empirical dives would be possible in fuller case study treatments, especially further interpretive-oriented interviewing. In our "partnership" case, for example, one of us (Bernstein) benefitted from "hanging out" during several expert group meetings including "friends of governance for sustainable development" and other UN Secretariat, government and NGO-sponsored meetings with officials, stakeholders, and diplomats between 2011–2019. These events, mostly hosted at the UN or in one case by the Chinese government in Beijing, also offered opportunities for informal discussions with, and observation of, interactions among diplomats, stakeholders, and officials in the lead-up and follow-up to the 2012 UN Conference on Sustainable Development (Rio + 20), the period of negotiation of the SDGs that followed, and early implementation of the SDGs, including during an early meeting of the UN's High Level Political Forum on Sustainable Development, the main UN body responsible for governance, review and follow-up of the SDGs. All these gatherings included policy and practical discussions on various aspects of the global partnership, partnerships, development finance, and, after 2015, SDG implementation, especially relating to institutional and practice reforms to implement sustainable development.[4]

Tight Coupling: COVID-19 and the Norm of Consular Support for Citizens Abroad

The tight-coupling scenario of social change describes situations where there is significant overlap between shared beliefs about appropriateness and standards for judging competence. Neither is completely static, but in this scenario they both evolve in a self-reinforcing way such that they are understood to be congruent throughout that process. We illustrate this dynamic by examining the relationship between the norm of consular support for citizens abroad and the practice of repatriation during the COVID-19 pandemic. While we focus primarily on the Canadian case, evidence suggests that many other states –

---

[4] Part of Bernstein's involvement stemmed from UN DESA commissioning him to write two consultant reports, the first in 2011 on Institutional Reform for Sustainable Development that fed into the Rio + 20 negotiations and a report on the role and function of the High-Level Forum on Sustainable Development immediately following its creation but before its first meeting (Bernstein and Brunnée 2011; Bernstein 2013).

including the United States, the United Kingdom, France, and several other EU countries – adjusted their approach to repatriation in similar ways during the pandemic. The most common change was a significant expansion in the scope and scale of repatriation efforts. Instead of repatriating a relatively small number of citizens from a particular country or region, many countries quickly brought tens of thousands of people home from across the globe.[5] Following Bueger, (2014, 2023) this empirical illustration relies primarily on praxiographic document analysis, treating international treaties and government documents as "access points" for deciphering practice and artefacts into which practices can be inscribed (2014, 398).

From an international legal perspective, sovereign states bear primary responsibility for ensuring the safety and security of citizens within their borders (UNHCR n.d.; International Commission on Intervention and State Sovereignty 2001, xi). However, this responsibility wanes when citizens travel abroad. For example, the Canadian Consular Services Charter notes that the decision to travel is a choice and it states that Canadians "are responsible for [their] personal safety abroad" (Government of Canada, 2016). Still, this does not mean that national governments are without obligations. The norm of consular support is one of the most well-established and widely recognized norms in international politics. More than 170 countries have signed the Vienna Convention on Consular Relations, which regulates a wide range of consular functions, such as "helping and assisting nationals" and "protecting ... the interests of the sending state and its nationals" (United Nations 1963; Crosbie 2018, 234). In addition to signing the Vienna Convention, some states have formally codified the consular support norm at the domestic level. Germany has a Consular Law that defines eligibility and governs the provision of consular support to citizens abroad (Government of Germany 1974). In Estonia, the constitution guarantees assistance for citizens abroad and provides a legal basis for consular support (Government of Estonia 2015). Other countries, including Canada, Australia, and the United Kingdom, have adopted consular charters (Government of Canada 2016; Government of the United Kingdom 2022; Australian Government 2022). These are public-facing documents that articulate expectations about when and how citizens can receive consular support. In virtually all cases, states are careful to manage expectations and place limits on what they can and cannot do for citizens abroad. Still, even countries like the Netherlands, which delegates the provision of consular

---

[5] In some cases, the mechanisms used were also new. For example, fifteen EU countries activated the European Union's Civil Protection Mechanism to assist with evacuations, the first time it had been used in response to a global pandemic. See Goldstein (2020), Foreign Affairs Committee (2020), Elzas (2020), European Parliament (2020).

support to their foreign ministry on a discretionary basis, acknowledge a duty to provide support for citizens abroad (Hoorens et al. 2019, 7–9). Put simply, when citizens are in distress outside their home state, that state is widely understood to have a duty to provide consular support (Okano-Heijmans 2010, 2; Graeger and Lindgren 2018, 189–190).[6]

This norm – a collective expectation about proper behaviour for sovereign states – has a long history and drives a longstanding element of diplomatic practice: the provision of consular assistance to citizens in need. In concrete terms, consular assistance can take many forms and includes a whole constellation of diplomatic practices. Officials from a state's embassy might replace lost or stolen travel documents; they might supply information about where to seek medical treatment or legal advice; they might intervene in cross-border child custody disputes; or they might undertake political negotiations aimed at securing the release of citizens taken hostage in a foreign country.[7] This diplomatic repertoire includes repatriation – a practice that involves facilitating a citizen's return to their country of origin, typically enacted in times of crisis. Repatriation can be undertaken for both individuals and groups. When citizens abroad fall ill, are caught amid a natural disaster, or are threatened by sudden political upheaval and cannot find their way home, states will often help repatriate them. Not surprisingly, there is significant variation in how states interpret their duty to provide consular support. Some prioritize assistance for individuals who are "most vulnerable," while others do not guarantee assistance for anyone with dual citizenship (Hoorens et al. 2019, 10–11). Still, the practice of repatriation – including mass repatriation during emergencies – has long been recognized as one way of enacting a state's duty to provide consular support (Graeger and Lindgren 2018).

When the World Health Organization (WHO) first characterized COVID-19 as a global pandemic in March 2020, governments around the world quickly urged their citizens to return home from abroad. Almost immediately, the Canadian Department of Global Affairs (GAC) launched what became the country's largest peacetime repatriation effort (May 2020, 1). The Canadian government had helped repatriate Canadians in distress on many previous occasions. The 2006 evacuation of citizens trapped in Lebanon owing to the war between Israeli defence forces and Hezbollah paramilitaries was a prime

---

[6] Graeger and Lindgren conceptualize this as a duty of care (DOC), a term derived from domestic tort law. We call it a duty to provide consular assistance – phrasing that does not have the same legal connotations – because the DOC concept remains underdeveloped in international law. We are grateful to Michaela Pedersen-Macnab for drawing this to our attention.

[7] See, for example, the Government of Canada's description of consular services Government of Canada, "About Consular Services." 2020. https://travel.gc.ca/assistance/emergency-info/consular (Accessed 31 March 2021).

example. Still, the Canadian government had never repatriated so many people at once, and never in response to a global pandemic. Repatriation for health reasons had taken place for individuals or small groups, but not for tens of thousands of people. The COVID-19 repatriation effort was therefore grounded in a new interpretation of the consular support norm, an interpretation that greatly expanded the scope and scale of the government's obligations. This, in turn, led to changes in the practice of repatriation. Three changes deserve particular attention: the rapid expansion of the repatriation effort; the adoption of new internal emergency management processes; and the increased level of political involvement. We examine each of these changes in turn.

While many elements of Canada's COVID-19 repatriation effort were familiar, it was notable for both its scale and scope. Between March and July 2020, more than 62,500 Canadians returned home on government-assisted flights (Government of Canada 2022). Prior to 2020, the country's largest mass repatriation effort was the voluntary evacuation of close to 14,300 people during the 2006 war in Lebanon (The Standing Senate Committee on Foreign Affairs and International Trade 2007, 1). Countries like the United Kingdom, Germany, and the United States also repatriated unprecedented numbers of people in the early days of the pandemic. The British government provided direct or indirect assistance – via chartered flights and ships, military transport, and government-facilitated commercial flights – to bring more than 190,000 people back to the United Kingdom (Government of the United Kingdom 2020). The German government chartered more than 260 flights to assist 260,000 citizens (Foreign Affairs Committee 2020, 7). The US State Department repatriated more than 100,000 US citizens and permanent residents in 137 countries during the first six months of 2020, a massive increase compared with the repatriation of just 6,000 people in the previous five years (United States Government 2021).

In addition to being larger, the COVID repatriation effort was also more geographically diffuse. From a Canadian perspective, a global health emergency had stranded thousands of Canadians in many places simultaneously and Global Affairs Canada was being asked to "evacuate the world," a scenario that staff had never dealt with or planned for (Government of Canada 2021). Starting in February 2020, the number of Canadians seeking consular assistance grew rapidly, with 117,100 calls and 23,700 emails received over the following six months. In response, GAC developed "a network of rolling and shadow embassies," which it used to coordinate logistics for 692 flights from 109 different countries to bring citizens and permanent residents back to Canada (May 2020, 1). The department also created a $20 million Emergency Loan Program for Canadians Outside Canada, an expanded version of the $150,000 Distressed Canadian Fund; when doing so, they dispensed with interest payments and much of the scrutiny that was normally part of the process to receive such a loan (May 2020, 18). To support these efforts, GAC re-assigned thousands of staff to work on repatriation, including 1,000 volunteers from other government departments: "nearly every available employee [was turned] into a full-time travel agent," with "staffers who used to write ministerial briefing notes ... booking hotels, buses, and flights" (CBC News 2020). This was not the first time that resources had been diverted to support a mass repatriation effort, but the amount of funding and the influx of employees from other departments added a new dimension, as did the wide geographic scope of the COVID repatriation effort.

The second change in GAC's approach to COVID-19 repatriation was linked to the increase in scale. Under normal circumstances, the department's Director of Emergency Operations responds to a crisis by mobilizing a small team and using the incident command model, which has pre-assigned roles and duties for operations, planning, logistics, reporting, finance, and administration. In 2019 alone, this team responded to the crash of Ethiopian Airlines flight 302, civil disorder in Khartoum and Port-au-Prince, hurricane Dorian, protests in Bolivia, and wildfires in Australia, among other crises. Yet the magnitude of the COVID-19 crisis quickly overwhelmed the team's capacity, and the incident command structure for emergencies was "blown up" and extended to become "the operating model for the entire department" (May 2020: 8). According to the Acting Assistant Deputy Minister for consular affairs, security and emergency management, GAC had "no choice but to elevate, escalate, expand, explode ... the whole incident command structure from a traditional model to one on steroids plus" (Reid Sirrs, quoted in May 2020, 9). For instance, key operational functions of the Emergency Watch and Response Centre were expanded and divided among GAC executives to cover 24-hour shifts. Air and sea teams were created to coordinate logistics for travellers on 109 flights and 197 cruise ships. When embassies abroad closed for the day, "shadow embassies" in Ottawa would take over fielding calls and emails (May 2020, 9). These innovations built on existing tools in the department's repatriation toolkit – underlining the fact that GAC was still understood to be engaging in a familiar practice – but they clearly constituted changes in that practice.

Finally, the COVID-19 repatriation effort was carried out with an unusually high level of political involvement. Typically, civil servants within GAC would take the lead on repatriation, including mass repatriation in response to large-scale crises. In this case, however, the Canadian Foreign Minister, Francois-Philippe Champagne, was "knee deep" in the politics and logistics of the COVID-19 repatriation effort (May 2020, 2). He took a variety of unusual steps, like texting the Peruvian Foreign Minister to secure landing rights for

Canadian planes, negotiating with chief executives from airlines and cruise lines, and intervening directly with his American and British counterparts to ensure that cruise ships could pass through the Panama Canal and eventually dock in Florida (Carbert 2020). This was due, in large part, to unique challenges posed by the pandemic, like large-scale closures of borders and air space. In the early days of the pandemic, things that would normally have been routine came to "depend on diplomacy because nothing [was] working on a normal commercial basis" (Carbert 2020). Again, it is not unprecedented for mass repatriation to have political dimensions that demand high-level diplomatic engagement. However, Champagne's degree of ongoing involvement – captured in the quip that he became "the travel agent of Canada" – was without precedent (Carbert 2020). The practice of repatriation endured, and remained linked to the consular support norm, but it was adjusted to meet the unique challenges associated with the pandemic.

Global Affairs Canada's approach to consular support and repatriation changed during the COVID-19 pandemic. The consular support norm was interpreted more broadly in response to a global health emergency. The practice of repatriation expanded in scope and scale. It came to rely on different institutional arrangements and depended on a much higher degree of political involvement. Even when taken together, these changes might seem minor. The COVID-19 repatriation process still bore a strong resemblance to previous mass repatriation efforts. As a result, GAC's activities were still recognized as repatriation – a familiar and well-established practice that enacts the consular support norm. While this might seem unremarkable, it is important to recognize that neither the norm nor the practice remained static. The consular support norm and the practice of repatriation evolved together and remained tightly coupled, at least in the early days of the pandemic.[8] This created a sense of continuity despite the fact that both the norm and the practice were changing.

It is too soon to say whether the changes described above will prove durable. While the COVID-19 pandemic gradually became a fact of life, and the Canadian government stopped its mass repatriation effort eight months after it began, there is some evidence that GAC will use new practices like establishing "shadow embassies" in response to other crises (Government of Canada 2021). Few would argue, however, that the consular support norm or the practice of repatriation has been fundamentally transformed. This is precisely the dynamic that our tight coupling scenario is meant to capture. It supports the view that norms and practices are both dynamic, and constantly changing in response to

---

[8] Later, after the government had explicitly warned Canadians not to travel abroad, there was a shift in policy. By November 2020 government support for repatriation was no longer available for those who had ignored government travel advisories (Jackson 2020).

new circumstances and situations, even if those changes are relatively minor and may, in some cases, fail to be perceived as change at all.

Disjunctures and Change: The Global Partnership for Development

Our third and fourth scenarios describe, respectively, the decoupling of a norm from novel practices over time and active contestation over the meaning, interpretation, and implementation of norms, or overt challenges to their legitimacy. Here we provide examples of both scenarios by examining the disjuncture between the norm of a "global partnership for development" and the practices of development associated with it, and their interplay over time. In this illustrative case, there is decoupling through the play of practice over time, followed by active, purposive, contestation. Note, our focus on the "partnership" norm is not meant to cover the entirety of global "development," which constitutes myriad practices, contested normative understandings, transactions, and policies involving a wide range of actors and "targets" of development across many geographies. Rather, our focus is specifically on the dominant governance framings, arrangements, and related practices of global development by major states from the North and South through the United Nations and its wider development system. The illustration also includes other major multilateral institutions that promote or engage in global development policies and practices, such as the OECD's Development Assistance Committee (DAC). Our framework reveals significant social change and how it occurred, which would be both masked and misunderstood if one focused only on development practices or the formal norm of "partnership."

We begin with the norm – albeit articulated initially as broad and aspirational – of "global partnership" as a baseline from which to observe change. Despite the dynamics we document, the norm itself – as a recognized social fact with prescriptive and constitutive qualities – has remained robust, being repeatedly and explicitly endorsed in major international initiatives since its original articulation in the Pearson Commission on International Development (1969) report: "Partners in Development." Yet, practices associated with the norm have shifted significantly toward multi-stakeholder "partnerships" – reflecting a more general move in practice away from an intergovernmental bargain to include a wider array of actors, especially the private sector. This shift occurred with little overt contestation (i.e., our scenario 3) until the disjuncture became widely visible in negotiations leading to the 2015 SDGs, reflecting our fourth scenario of change only in this later period. An observable pressure for congruence gradually emerged but is still underway and its future trajectory is uncertain.

The norm of "partnership," as identifying the appropriate way to understand and practice global development, was crystalized originally in the 1969 Pearson Commission. One of its chief aims was to shift the discourse around development to one of a "cooperative" partnership among donor and recipient states, with "reciprocal rights and obligations," particularly regarding foreign aid to combat poverty (Commission on International Development 1969, 127). While donors would be responsible for more predictable aid flows and, as the norm evolved, for working with recipients to improve performance and aid effectiveness, the ultimate responsibility for development policies should lie with recipient countries, an idea currently articulated as "country ownership" (Clarke 2003; Black 2020). The partnership norm also became linked to the 0.7 percent GDP/GNI target for donor countries to contribute to overseas development assistance, entrenched formally as a UN-sponsored target in a 1970 General Assembly Resolution following the recommendation of the Pearson report.

Consistent with all our scenarios of change, the normative understanding of "partnership" evolved as it became articulated in various forums and statements of principles; it was always aspirational, and frequently did not match a "technocratic sense of the term in practice" (Black 2020, 116). However, the basic principles of a global partnership – rooted in cooperative bilateral relationships, shared responsibility, and a focus on aid, trade including market access, debt relief and access to technology – remained remarkably robust and understood as an expectation of the aid and development relationship between North and South. By the 1990s, "the partnership discourse began to dominate mainstream policy," particularly in the DAC of major donors in the OECD (Clarke 2003, 309). The outcomes of major UN processes such as the 2002 Conference on Financing for Development's Monterrey Consensus (UN 2003) as well as the discourse of multilateral development institutions such as the World Bank also consistently reflected the norm. While the specific emphasis evolved – from a focus on development targets in the mid-1990s to "aid effectiveness" in the 2000s as guided by the OECD's 2005 Paris Declaration – the core focus remained on bilateral cooperative relationships, donor coordination, shared responsibilities and developing country ownership (Clarke 2003; Black 2020; Brown 2020). Moreover, even while practices of development finance and aid always included non-state actors to some degree, the partnership norm firmly articulates state-to-state responsibilities rooted in a sovereignty-based bargain.

The language of "global partnership" also gradually gained traction as underpinning North–South bargains over responsibilities for sustainable development as the UN's development agenda evolved in that direction after the publication of the Brundtland Commission report (WCED 1987). For example, it appears in the 1992 Rio Declaration, Principle 7, the most general statement of the core equity norm of "common but differentiated responsibilities" and respective capabilities, that now underpins many international environmental agreements (UN 1992): "States shall co-operate in a spirit of global partnership to conserve, protect and restore the health and integrity of the Earth's ecosystem ... [and] have common but differential responsibilities ... ." The reference to partnership remains firmly focused on the responsibilities of states to address common problems, but also on states' differential responsibilities to each other, mainly indicated by the greater responsibility of countries in the North commensurate with their relative capabilities and economic position.[9]

This broader understanding coalesced in Millennium Development Goal (MDG) 8, to "develop a global partnership for development," the UN's initial attempt to bring norms and practices into congruence by explicitly broadening the focus beyond aid. Its targets build upon many of the recommendations of the Pearson Commission, including an emphasis on a non-discriminatory trade and financial system and access to markets, increasing foreign aid, addressing developing country debt, and increasing access to technology, updated to focus especially on essential medicines and communication technology (UN "Millennium Development Goals Indicators").

Despite the absence of overt contestation over MDG 8, in the background was a growing disjuncture between the aspirational norms of "global partnership" and practices of development, especially around the role of the private sector. Rather than reflecting a state–state bargain, implementation of development goals increasingly emphasized domestic reform, private investment, and a move towards multi-stakeholder public-private "partnerships" in recognition of the limits of multilateralism and bilateral aid and the need to mobilize stakeholders and private finance.

A full account of these trends in development practice is beyond the scope of this Element. Instead, we focus particularly on the rise of multi-stakeholder partnerships because of the way this practice directly interacted with the norm of global partnership. The broader origin story of the rise of partnerships is also a complicated one, with multiple sources. Various literatures highlight, and debate the relative importance of, the discourse of "business managerialism" that started to gain traction in the mid twentieth century and the related idea of taking account of the interests of stakeholders and not just shareholders; the championing of these ideas by prominent entrepreneurial business leaders like Klaus Schwab who amplified them through globally influential networks like

---

[9] For a fuller discussion of the framing and limits of this responsibility, especially in reference to current capabilities and the lack of acceptance of liability or historical responsibility, see Bernstein 2021.

the World Economic Forum; the desire to mobilize and engage the private sector in development that grew especially from the 1990s onward and that the UN took up in the 2000s; and, beginning in the 1980s, the increase in demands from civil society and many international organizations for more inclusive decision-making and accountability to those affected by development policies and programs (see Raymond and DeNardis 2015; Higham et al. 2024, section 3; Taggart and Abraham 2024 for a range of accounts). While a fuller case-study treatment might document these practices and origins in more detail, for our more limited and illustrative purposes here, the relevant story is how they made their way into the global development field, which we trace below, along with the resulting dynamics of change.

The overt promotion of partnerships picked up steam in the early 2000s. For example, the most significant outcome of the UN's 2002 World Summit on Sustainable Development in Johannesburg was the adoption of 348 public-private partnerships to implement sustainable development in the wake of poor progress in intergovernmental cooperation (UN 2002; Bäckstrand and Kylsäter 2014). While both the Monterrey Consensus and the Johannesburg Plan of Implementation elaborated on the concept of partnership for development and its emphasis on aid, trade and technology, they simultaneously promoted multi-stakeholder partnerships (UN 2002; United Nations 2003; UN 2013, 3). However, neither explicitly linked the two concepts.

The explicit promotion of "partnerships" as a means of implementation continued as a subtext of the evolving understanding of "global partnership" in the mid-2000s but remained treated in parallel and as supplemental. UN General Assembly resolutions, beginning in 2000, under the title "Towards global partnerships," regularly started appearing to mandate the inclusion of an item on partnerships in the UNGA's regular sessions. However, these resolutions, starting in 2001, began "*Underlining* the fact that the resources contributed by the relevant partners, in particular the private sector, should be a complement to, not a substitute for, governmental resources," while acknowledging their increasingly important role to achieve development goals including the MDGs (United Nations 2001, emphasis in original). Rather than challenge the norm of global partnership in MDG 8, these resolutions reflected a disjuncture in how to "do" development globally, recognizing that in practice partnership increasingly meant arrangements and activities of wider arrays of actors beyond states.

In the years leading up to the negotiation of the 2015 SDGs, the disjuncture became harder to ignore. For example, the outcome of the 2011 Busan (Korea) high-level forum of the OECD's DAC undermined the focus on aid effectiveness and instead "called for a new more inclusive Global Partnership" to take over from the OECD's management of the partnership agenda (Brown 2020). The resulting "Global Partnership for Effective Development Cooperation," itself a multi-stakeholder partnership, functioned mainly as a platform for sharing of best practices with less direct impact on development policy. Nonetheless, it signalled shifts in practices by replacing the "binary vision of Northern donors and Southern recipients" with one that emphasized the perspective "of a wide variety of actors, with often overlapping roles" (Brown 2020, 1239; Taggart 2022).

By the time governments negotiated the SDGs, their positions reflected a disjuncture that had already occurred. Yet the norm of "global partnership" remained powerfully alive in SDG 17: "Strengthen the means of implementation and revitalize the Global Partnership for Sustainable Development." On the one hand, the targets of SDG 17 include an even more detailed list covering longstanding themes of partnership including objectives on finance, aid, trade, and "systemic issues" of policy and institutional coherence. On the other hand, a new item appears, included under "systemic issues": multi-stakeholder partnerships "to support the achievement of the Sustainable Development Goals in all countries, in particular developing countries" (UN General Assembly 2015). And, the elaboration of means of implementation in Agenda 2030, the full UNGA resolution (A/RES/70/1) that contains the SDGs, further emphasizes that the "revitalized Global Partnership will facilitate an intensive global engagement in support of implementation of all the Goals and targets, bringing together Governments, civil society, the private sector, the United Nations system and other actors and mobilizing all available resources" (UN General Assembly 2015). Meanwhile, the public facing UN website and publicity, which use a shorthand for each goal, identifies goal 17 as "partnerships for the goals" (United Nations, n.d. a). Likewise, the main UN sponsored platform for implementation – until recently called the "partnership platform" although now called the "SDG actions platform" – is a registry of over 7,800 "voluntary policies, commitments, multi-stakeholder partnerships and other initiatives made by governments, the UN system and a broad range of stakeholders . . . ." (United Nations, n.d. b). Empirical analyses similarly provide strong evidence of the exponential rise of multi-stakeholder partnerships in development practice since the end of the Cold War, arguably now the "preferred modality of [international] cooperation in development" (Reinsberg and Westerwinter 2021, 61, 70–73). While the exact number and categorization of partnerships in international registries are debated, empirical analyses widely agree that multi-stakeholder partnerships "are proliferating as never before" (Bull and McNeill 2019, 466), while "elements constitutive of multi-stakeholderism – such as non-state participation, corporate partnerships, voluntarism, and informality – are regarded as the 'default mode of global decision-making' [and have been] termed 'The Great Takeover'" (Taggart and Abraham 2024, 355, quoting Buxton 2019, 12; Manahan and Kumar, 2021).

These various official statements, analyses, and observations recognize what was already occurring in practice. While there are different ways of counting development assistance, comparing "private development assistance" to "official development assistance" over the last thirty years is one good proxy for the shift in practices observed here. The former refers to "grants by private voluntary agencies and non-government organizations (NGOs) ... defined as transfers for development made by private voluntary agencies [including private foundations] or corporate and NGOs in cash, goods or services for which no payment is required" (OECD n.d. a), while the latter is the traditional measure of aid, which "includes activities [bilateral or multilateral] carried out with the economic development and welfare of developing countries as their main objective. It is a measure of donor [country] effort, including grants and grant equivalents of concessional loans." To give a sense of the trend, in 1992, total ODA from OECD countries was $87.5 billion, and private development assistance was $9.8 billion (all amounts USD), or equal to about 11.2% of ODA. In 2002, ODA, after a dip in the late 1980s, had risen to just below 1992 levels, at $86.7 billion but private development assistance had risen to $14.2, or equal to 16.5 % of ODA. By 2022 (the latest year for which figures are available), ODA was $210.7 billion (which is probably inflated as it reflects large increases in the wake of Covid-19 and the Ukraine war) while private development assistance had risen to $55.8 billion, or equivalent to 26.5% of ODA (OECD n.d. a and n.d. b). Most analyses agree that the role of the private sector in such statistics is probably underreported. This, along with the absolute rise in partnerships, makes the trend in practices clear.

Given the growing visibility of the disjuncture between norm and practices leading up to negotiations over the SDGs, more overt contestation occurred consistent with our scenario 4. Many developing countries advocated a "solidarist" set of values consistent with partnership understood as shared responsibility, and pushed beyond even the focus on aid, trade, and technology to advocate for developed countries to take the lead in providing the means of implementation (Pouliot and Thérien 2018, author observations at UN meetings). They also contested the narrower understanding of partnership as a relationship between donor and recipients, arguing it should be interpreted to include structural reforms in global institutions (Fukuda-Parr and Muchhala 2020, 7–8). Many developed countries, however, resisted the inclusion of institutional reform, instead emphasizing interpretations of country ownership focused on the need to increase domestic sources of finance, the role of the private sector, and more general support of a "national duty" or responsibility understanding of ownership, reinforcing a primary role for partnerships (Pouliot and Thérien 2018).

On a general level, SDG 17 explicitly acknowledged that "global partnership" included a wide range of actors beyond governments, recognizing that practices of finance for development already had shifted to include major roles for remittances, philanthropy, and foreign direct and other private investment in addition to foreign aid and multilateral finance mechanisms. Specifically, it views multi-stakeholder partnerships as a primary means of implementation. "The MDGs – widely seen as top-down and technocratic – conceived of partnership as official development assistance, but the SDGs differ in their definition of partnerships by institutionalizing a clear role for nonstate actors" (Higham et al. 2024). But simply looking at this shift from the perspective of the rise of partnerships misses the massive change in global development and the contestation over the previous normative consensus. This is not "norm-governed" change, to use Ruggie's (1982) terminology, but norm-transformative, even as official documents and decisions continue to state the same formal norm. Meanwhile, some analysts have implied that the normative transformation under the SDGs was all but complete. For example, for Long, Clough, and Rietig (2022, 28), "Partnerships are a watchword – a 'metanorm' [quoting Sondermann and Ulbert 2021] of the SDG framework." Similarly, Taggart and Abraham (2024, 356) argue that "Agenda 2030 situates multistakeholderism as the *sine qua non* approach to global problem solving," and they identify it as a "norm" in the sense of "specifying that global public problems *ought* to be addressed by those actors who *affect*, or are *affected by*, these problems." Similarly, United Nations publications have also been quite explicit in this normative goal, including their desire to make partnerships "the new normal" in implementing the SDGs (Stibbe and Prescott 2020). Tellingly, and consistent with our framework, Taggart and Abraham (2024, 256) also make clear that

> configuring multistakeholderism as a norm, rather than as a practice or institution (c.f. Raymond and DeNardis, 2015), allows us to capture the normative pull to include multiple affected parties in global governance despite the diverse institutional forms it may take in practice. Thus, rather than define multistakeholderism in terms of its institutional composition (i.e., decision-making procedures or rules) we pose it as a broader norm concerning how 'good' governance ought to proceed.

Our approach, which differentiates norms and practices and traces how they each evolve, thus has the advantage of laying bare disjunctures between them, while still acknowledging their relational qualities, their dynamism, and the social change that these tensions create.

To put an even finer point on the tension, the UN discourse sees partnerships – or the multi-stakeholderism norm that arguably underpins them – as encompassed by the "partnership norm" and simply the preferred way to implement it. As Long, Clough, and Rietig (2022, 27) state, referencing Agenda 2030, "This partnership is partly envisaged as an agreement about *interstate* cooperation but is also a commitment to a 'partnership of partnerships' at different scales among the widest possible range of stakeholders." Given the confusion and shift away from responsibility and accountability among states entailed in this social change, it is not surprising that the burgeoning literature on development partnerships has focused extensively on questions of legitimacy, accountability and the need for new mechanisms, such as "meta-governance," or "orchestration," to achieve it (e.g., Bäckstrand and Kylsäter 2014; Kramarz 2020; Long, Clough, and Rietig 2022; Higham et al. 2024).

The apparent new normative consensus that links "partnership" with "partnerships" masks contestation, however, with many governments in the South viewing Northern states' support for partnerships as "a Trojan horse to favour the private sector" (Thérien and Pouliot 2020, 627). In reaction, the G77 and China have explicitly downplayed multi-stakeholderism in favour of an intergovernmental approach to "global partnership" (G77 and China 2015, author observations at the 2014 HLPF meetings).

Simultaneously, even as the norm of "aid effectiveness" has clearly weakened (Brown 2020), older extant norms continue to be articulated in UN development organizations and meetings by many states in the Global South. Meanwhile, buy in, especially of the major emerging economies (China, Brazil, India, and South Africa in particular), to the OECD's Global Partnership for Effective Development Cooperation has been minimal (Brown 2020; Taggart and Abraham 2024), suggesting it has especially failed as a forum to promote south-south cooperation and highlighting ongoing contestation – from multiple directions – over roles and norms to govern development assistance or the implementation of the SDGs. The critiques of partnerships and increasing pressures for accountability suggest similar inchoateness on their governance, leading to a messy and uncertain evolution as the disjuncture grows.

In sum, the changing meaning of "partnership for development" epitomizes our scenario 3 where similar normative language is used to justify an increasingly obvious disjuncture with practices of development. Elements of our scenario 4 – overt contestation – became manifest as the norms around development have become increasingly inchoate. It is not simply the rhetoric around "partnership" (understood as a North-South bargain) versus multi-stakeholder partnerships, but also that the governance of development itself has become contested as the practices have rapidly evolved. It has become nearly impossible to identify an agreed-upon set of norms under such circumstances, though the social change is evident, as we have documented. Taggart (2022, 905), for example, calls the current period an interregnum, noting "'old' institutions responsible for cooperation – such as the OECD's ... DAC – face declining relevance and efficacy due to uncertainties and contestations from within, and 'new' actors and ideological challenges from without ... In response ... new institutional innovations have emerged – such as the multi-stakeholder Global Partnership for Effective Development Cooperation." The latter's failure to articulate or entrench, let alone develop strong compliance mechanisms to encourage, a clear set of norms is emblematic of the disjuncture scenario. Absent our framework, this situation could easily be misread as indicating normative stability or decline instead of revealing the social change that has occurred owing to the disjuncture.

Future research might examine whether this disjuncture leads to an increasing pull towards congruence, though the institutional fragmentation of the development landscape may militate against that. One thing is clear, however. The old meaning of partnership for development no longer applies and new practices, as delineated above, are not only clearly in evidence, but also increasingly understood to be performed "competently."

5 Conclusion

The primary purpose of this Element has been to develop and demonstrate a productive way to make sense of change and continuity in global politics through an exploration of various dynamics of *social change*. To advance understandings of social change, we have argued that it is useful to bring norms and practices into dialogue. While there is now a flourishing literature bridging these once-bifurcated concepts, we uncovered several important debates that remain. Via engagement with those debates, we developed four analytical scenarios of social change. These scenarios foreground the varied potential relationships between norms and practice. We have sought to place both norms and practice and their interrelationship on scholars' radar early in their research process such that they may structure their inquiry, shape new research questions, and guide the study of different empirical phenomena. As we have demonstrated, by treating both norms and practice as analytically productive focal points, rather than starting our analysis with a focus on one or the other, we have advanced one means of minimizing conceptual and methodological entrapment and opened more fruitful, productive means of exploring continuity and change in global politics.

In this final section, we conclude in three steps. First, we summarize our core claims, reviewing the ongoing debates about social change, articulating the

Norms, Practices, and Social Change in Global Politics 51

analytical approach we build from them, and surveying the conclusions drawn from the preceding empirical illustrations. In doing so, we aim to underscore our central claim: that norms and practices are interrelated in varied and important ways, and that stability and change in a complex social world are the products of varied interactions between them. Second, moving beyond the illustrative cases of global governance in earlier sections, we show the wider applicability and value of our scenarios for contemporary debates in global politics about major governance and security issues. To concretize these claims, we offer schematic illustrations that centre on contemporary challenges to the liberal international order and the implications of Russia's war in Ukraine. Third, we conclude by offering a few suggestions for future research.

Core Claims

The early promise of research on norms centred on scholars' ability to use the concept to identify and explain change in global politics, particularly those dynamics missed by rationalist and materialist theories that neglected social dimensions of change. A focus on norms helped account for major, easily observable changes, including the end of the Cold War and the unravelling of the Soviet Union, decolonization, diffusion and contestation over human rights and liberalism, and the emergence of new modes of governance on issues ranging from weapons prohibitions to climate change and development (see Katzenstein 1996; Jurkovich 2020). While valuable and productive, early norms research, as we explored in Section 1, has been widely critiqued by scholars attentive to the more subtle, relational, and internalized aspects of stability and change in global politics (see Drieschova, Bueger, and Hopf 2022). Practice theorists of all kinds have rejected what they view as the reification of norms in IR scholarship, particularly arguments that present norms as static social things. A growing literature examines the contested character of norms and the dynamic ways they are adapted or localized across contexts (Acharya 2004; Wiener 2004, 2009; Krook and True 2010; Zwingel 2016; Deitelhoff and Zimmermann 2019; Wiener and Orchard 2024). But for practice theorists, even such moves are insufficient. They argue that a focus on meaningful patterns of action – or practices – better captures the social forces and behaviours through which global politics is enacted. This focus on practices, they argue, better allows examinations of stability and change than do assumptions about the static content or dynamics of norms. However, much of the focus of practice scholarship has been geared towards unearthing and accounting for surprising continuities in social relations; practice theorists often highlight how established modes of doing and thinking recreate patterns in global politics over long periods. The result of this focus on continuity, which we have been party to as well (e.g., Glas and Laurence 2022), is a tendency to downplay agency and to see change – apart from incremental and unintentional shifts in practices themselves – as both exogenously driven and rather rare. In this Element, we have combined a focus on norms as fluid and processual qualities of global politics with close attention to international practices. The value of our ontological move in combining these two focal points, while privileging neither norms nor practices over the other, is to maintain the focus on social change while also illustrating several scenarios through which it occurs, scenarios that would otherwise be missed. As we showed in Section 2, to build those scenarios, we first examined four major debates in the existing literature around how to observe change, whether norms are things or dynamic processes, the role of agency, and the conditions that make change possible in the first place. From our focus on norms and practice and survey of these debates, we then articulated and developed various analytical scenarios. The scenarios centred on the interactions between practice and the normative understandings practitioners work under, capturing elements of the fundamental play of agency and structure that underpins almost all theories of social change. As we outlined in Section 3, we see four analytical scenarios of potential social change, ranging from a tight coupling of norms and practice to outright rejection.

Our first scenario is well-established in constructivist literature. This scenario describes a "tight coupling" between norms and practices. Here, we can observe a substantial overlap between standards for judging competence and shared beliefs about appropriate behaviour. This does not mean, however, that norms and practices remain static. Rather, tight coupling describes a situation in which they gradually change together. This scenario underscores the frequently entangled relationship between both norms and practices, and it nicely captures the dynamics we described in Section 4, as countries reinterpreted a longstanding international norm – of consular assistance for citizens abroad – in ways that allowed for a significant expansion in the scope and scale of repatriation efforts during the COVID-19 pandemic. Instead of repatriating a relatively small number of people from one country or region, many countries quickly brought tens of thousands of citizens home from across the globe. The consular support norm and the practice of repatriation both changed in meaningful ways, but tight coupling between the norm and the practice created a sense of continuity nevertheless. In contrast, our second scenario describes situations where gaps arise between norms and practices because practices are performed "incompetently," through misunderstanding, error, or inability to perform competently.

This scenario describes situations where there is some inadvertent disjuncture, and with variable effects on norms and practice over time. If practices are revised such that they are again perceived as competent, then this brief disjuncture may serve to reinforce a norm, re-establishing expectations and set ways of doing things by righting 'incorrect' practices. If practices remain incompetent for long periods of time, however, the underlying norm may erode or transform in meaningful ways. While change via scenario 2 is, in our view, very plausible, this scenario is the most speculative of the four; we believe it is important for researchers to consider it as one pathway by which social change might occur. However, we do not fully develop this scenario empirically because a review of the secondary literature suggests that it is the one least likely to yield meaningful change.

Our third scenario also speaks to disjunctures. In this scenario, unacknowledged disjunctures arise between norms and practices as standards for judging competence and shared beliefs about appropriateness gradually drift apart through the ongoing "play" of practice. In this scenario practices continue to be interpreted as consistent with established norms, even as they manifestly diverge over time. We illustrate this scenario with the disjuncture between the apparently stable norm of "Partnership for Development" despite several changes in the practices of development and its governance while ostensibly still covered by the norm. As the social change in this realm of governance became harder to ignore, overt contestation eventually erupted, most prominently in the negotiations of the SDGs. Along with this contestation, norms and governance arrangements are under increasing pressure to change, illustrative of our scenario 4. That scenario speaks to change through purposeful acts of resistance and transgression, dynamics recognized well in accounts of overt norm contestation.

As we make clear, these scenarios are not exhaustive, nor are they mutually exclusive. Rather, they serve a typological purpose in our thinking about different ways by which norms and practice are interrelated, and pathways through which social change might occur. They take relational critiques of the norms literature seriously without jettisoning the concept of a norm altogether. While the utility of our approach is clear from the cases surveyed, its value is not confined to them. Rather, we can extend our analytical focus to see how thinking through these scenarios can offer insight into the dynamics of social change or continuity in a series of unfolding issues in global politics today.

Extending the Analytical Focus

One important payoff of the ontology and method in our approach is to differentiate types and patterns of social change that are currently left vague or underspecified in literatures on norms and practice. In this way, our approach can be valuable to scholars trying to analyze social change across major issue areas today. Our empirical illustrations in Section 4 centre on discrete instances of social change in areas of global health, development, and sustainable development governance. Here, however, we outline how our approach is relevant to "bigger" questions about global order, using examples from Russia's ongoing war in Ukraine. In what follows, we do not offer a complete analysis, but we demonstrate the value of adopting our scenarios in thinking about some of the most expansive questions about change in global politics.

On February 24th, 2022, the Russian armed forces launched air strikes across Ukraine and Russian troops crossed the Ukrainian border in what many international observers described as a form of blatant military aggression not seen in Europe since the Second World War (Graham-Harrison et al. 2022). Beyond the invasion's impact on Russian-Ukrainian relations, many experts believe it signalled a major change in global politics. But what type of change? Scholars and analysts of all kinds have grappled with this question and tried to pinpoint what changes, exactly, have been sparked by the invasion and the large-scale war that followed. The answer, of course, is that the invasion has caused many different types of change. To make sense of them, a nuanced and multi-faceted framework is needed to make different types of change visible and provide versatile concepts for analyzing them.

To date, debates about changes related to the invasion have centred on implications for the European Union (EU), the North Atlantic Treaty Organization (NATO), and for what is commonly referred to as the liberal international order. Our analytical scenarios offer flexible tools for analyzing change in all three of these areas.

First, observers and practitioners alike have debated changes in or of the EU because of the war (e.g., Cohen 2023; Scholz 2023). These accounts highlight the emergence of new or renewed ideas and novel forms of EU practice, which together suggest a "paradigm shift" in the character of the organization itself (Meister 2022). According to many observers, Europe has been "changed forever" in the face of the war; "no event has transformed the continent more profoundly since the end of the Cold War, and there is no going back now" (Cohen 2023). In this view, an important social change has occurred and is apparent in thinking and behaviours of EU officials and member states. On the first count, the invasion of Ukraine sparked new ideas in the minds of EU and member state officials – a new "mentality" (Cohen 2023). These new ideas concern the European relationship with Russia, the potential for war on the continent, and the bounds of what the EU could or should do as an organization with its own foreign policy in response to the aggression to its east. For observers, new ideas prompted new behaviours, too. The organization and its members have been "galvanized into an immense effort to save liberty in Ukraine, a freedom widely seen as synonymous with its own" (Cohen 2023). These efforts are visible in the collective sanctions from the EU (and others), through the EU coordination mechanism, and in the provision of lethal military aid to Ukraine. They are also visible in the assertive and militarized orientation of leading members, as exemplified by German Chancellor Olaf Scholz' 2022 *Zeitenwende* speech and French President Emmanuel Macron's posturing towards a more militarized EU. The latter included Macron's stating the potential to send European troops to Ukraine (France 24 2024). Other signals of change in the EU itself include visits to Kyiv from European Commission President Ursula von der Leyen and European Council President Charles Michel.

Our framework can help scholars make sense of such changes. Conceptualizing them in terms of both norms and practice – which, together, make up the component parts of institutions – captures dynamics that would be invisible if these events were only studied through the lens of norm change or practice change. For instance, the Common Foreign and Security Policy (CFSP) was a core pillar of the post-Maastricht EU, one that laid out norms governing the Union's external relations with non-members. The Treaty of Maastricht called for the EU to "assert its identity on the international scene," through a common foreign and security policy that promoted peace internationally and addressed "all questions related to the security of the Union" (European Union, 1992). Yet there is wide agreement that implementation of the CFSP fell short of the normative expectations articulated in 1992. Despite pursuing integration with enthusiasm in many other fields, EU states were, in practice, reluctant to surrender sovereignty in this area of "high politics" (Sjursen 2005, 34). The Treaty of Lisbon rearticulated norms related to the CFSP – improving the coherence of EU external relations was ostensibly one of its "central themes" – and it established an EU High Representative for Foreign Affairs and Security Policy (European Peacebuilding Liaison Office n.d.). Still, many of the treaty's provision were not implemented because states feared a "loss of control" in these fields (Troszczynska-van Genderen 2015). Put differently, there was a disconnect between diplomatic practice and formal EU norms related to defence and security cooperation. This is consistent with scenario 4, in which "transgressive" practices are linked to overt normative contestation. What we now see, however, is a pull toward congruence between EU norms and the diplomatic practices of member states. While much of the support that Europe provides to Ukraine comes through bilateral channels, we also see a growing willingness to have the EU play a central coordinating role. The long-term impact of this "pull" is uncertain. The critical point is that examining either norms or practices in isolation would not capture the interplay between a codified EU norm and the EU's evolving diplomatic practices in the face of Russian military aggression.

Relatedly, many observers have debated how to make sense of the war's effects on NATO. Most believe change is afoot as the organization grapples with how to respond, and that existing norms and practices are under threat or in need of purposeful renewal. Again, however, it is not entirely clear what change is occurring and why. In one view, the war has changed NATO by compelling the organization and its members to return to established norms and practices and has, in doing so, empowered the organization with a renewed unity and purpose. This change would be in line with our scenario 1. In 1999, the Alliance adopted a new Strategic Concept that called for it to recognize unconventional, transnational threats, respond to insecurity and instability outside its collective borders, and prepare for "non-Article 5 activities," an expanded focus that did not always sit well with members in Eastern Europe who remained wary of Russia (Davis 2010, 36). This kicked off two decades of experimentation with new practices, including peace enforcement and post-conflict stabilization in Kosovo and counter-insurgency warfare in Afghanistan. Now, however, NATO is supposedly back in more familiar territory. The Ukraine war has compelled "NATO back to basics – containing Russian power and imperium" (Erlanger 2022). Change, in this view, is less about new forms of practice, than it is a return to previously central norms for the organization. Renewed fears about the "democratic cohesion of NATO," the territorial sovereignty of member states, like Poland, and the possibility of large-scale war in Europe beyond Ukraine, have brought a reorientation in NATO practice and a return to "the DNA of NATO" in deterring and containing Russian aggression (Erlanger 2022).

At first glance, this might seem like a move back toward congruence between traditional NATO norms and the Alliance's day-to-day practices. For some in this view, a realignment of NATO practice with established norms has helped restore unity within the organization. In the words of former United States Permanent Representative to NATO Ivo Daalder, "all the divisions are dissolved, at least for today" (Erlanger 2022). Yet our framework highlights another possibility. NATO's collective defence norm – articulated in Article 5 of the Washington Treaty and described as a "unique and enduring principle that binds [NATO] members together" – establishes a clear expectation that states will treat an attack on any member of the Alliance as an attack against all (North Atlantic Treaty Organization 2023a). Yet Ukraine is not a member of the Alliance. It remains a "partner country" and some members have questioned whether staunch NATO support for a non-member is really in keeping with longstanding NATO norms. In this reading, the pivot to contain Russian expansionism has driven a wedge between member states and created a disjuncture between new NATO practices and the norms invoked to justify them, dynamics consistent with our third scenario. Most notably, officials from the Alliance's democratic and authoritarian states have long disagreed about how much support for Ukraine is appropriate, divisions further exacerbated by Donald Trump's return to the presidency in 2025. Similarly, for some members, the return of naked Russian expansion prompted a logical expansion of the organization's membership, while this has been questioned by others. This is most apparent in Turkey's slowing of Sweden's accession to NATO and in Hungary's stark questioning of eventual Ukrainian membership (Cook 2023). Again, there is quiet disagreement – again consistent with scenario 3 – about whether the Alliance's "open door policy," which states the organization should welcome any European country in a position to undertake the commitments and obligations of membership, is consistent with NATO enlargement as it is currently being practiced (North Atlantic Treaty Organization 2023b). Our framework makes it much easier to discern these dynamics and explore the process by which social change does or does not occur.

Third, the invasion has raised wider questions about stability, change, and the liberal international order. Indeed, there is a burgeoning academic literature on geopolitical change, multipolarity, the rise of nationalism and authoritarianism, and challenges to the liberal international order that has played such a central role in global politics since the end of the Second World War. In some respects, Russia's invasion of Ukraine is just one more event driving such questions. Scholars have documented the varied pressures on liberalism from multiple sources, including both Russia and China, and noted shifting norms and practices around multilateralism and international law (e.g., Ikenberry 2018; Abrahamsen, Andersen, and Sending 2019; Lake, Clough, and Rietig 2021). However, the Russian invasion and ongoing responses to the war from China and other states have added greater urgency to debates about whether the liberal world order can survive, and how global politics might change as a result. Most notable here are questions about the dissolution of norms around territorial sovereignty. While respect for sovereignty has never been absolute (Krasner 1999), deliberate attempts at territorial conquest are relatively rare – the practice of territorial conquest has long been considered unjustifiable from a normative perspective (Finnemore 2003). Not since Iraq's invasion of Kuwait in 1990 has such a stark rejection of a state's territorial integrity been witnessed. On this point, Fazal (2022) adopts the lens of norms and practice to examine the changes underway that followed the Russian invasion. Her analysis is in line with the dynamics articulated in our fourth scenario.

In her view, the Russia's invasion of Ukraine demonstrates both a rejection of the post-WWII "norm against territorial conquest," as well as "bedrock principles of international law" (Fazal 2022). In rejecting these established, if imperfect, post-war norms, Russian behaviour signals a change in great power practice through deliberate contestation of key principles of the liberal international order. It also portends the return of the long-rejected practice of territorial conquest. Following Fazal, other observers also question whether this change in practice will spill over elsewhere. Indeed the "thawed" conflict between Armenia and Azerbaijan on Russia's periphery may point to such a dynamic already (Baer 2022) and observers have raised questions about an emboldened China over its disputed border with India (Roy-Chaudhury 2023) or its interest in forceful unification of Taiwan (Osnos 2022).

Adopting the lens of norms and practice, as Fazal does, is valuable, but our framework provides tools for discerning other, more complex dynamics. For instance, the Russian government relies on a variety of different (sometimes contradictory) pretexts to justify the war. Two deserve particular attention in debates about the war's implications for sovereignty norms. First, Russian officials sometimes respond to criticism by claiming that Ukraine is not really a state, a claim that would – by implication – mean that the government in Kyiv cannot credibly claim a right to sovereign autonomy or territorial integrity (University of Rochester News Center 2022). Second, Russian President Vladimir Putin has claimed that Russia's "special military operation" in Ukraine is necessary to protect people who are "facing humiliation and genocide perpetrated by the Kyiv regime" (Office of the President of Russia 2022). While both claims have been widely dismissed as baseless, they are interesting because instead of rejecting sovereignty norms outright, they seek to justify the invasion in ways that are consistent with existing international rules. The first claim suggests that the territorial integrity norm simply does not apply to Ukraine. The second taps into norms articulated in the Genocide Convention and the Responsibility to Protect (R2P) doctrine, which suggest that military intervention may be justifiable to prevent mass atrocities (International Commission on Intervention and State Sovereignty 2001). This reluctance to overtly contest sovereignty norms resembles scenario 3 more than scenario 4. Going forward, prospects for social change will depend on whether the invasion comes to be viewed as a successful challenge to sovereignty norms and whether an alternative model of world order exists. As Fazal (2022) notes, much of the global community has contested these normative and practice changes through economic sanctions and both humanitarian and military aid to Ukraine. In her view, then, "countries are largely united in their determination to protect the [sovereignty] norm." There is no doubt that sovereignty norms and the liberal world order are under pressure, but they may yet prove resilient and surprisingly adaptable.

Yet, the apparent shift in US policy under President Trump to accept violations of those norms demonstrates how disjunctures can also shift to overt contestation and a pull toward congruence that brings a more radical change.

Conclusions and Future Research

We see an array of possible avenues of future inquiry to advance theory, building on the analytic scaffolding of our framework, and extending empirical investigations beyond our limited focus here on global governance and organizational dynamics.

The first involves expanding and adding nuance to our scenarios themselves, especially scenario 2, which remains more speculative. For example, future work might aim to further specify the core mechanisms of change that characterize each scenario and the conditions that give rise to different types of change. This would enable a more detailed account of similarities and differences between the scenarios and enhance their utility for scholars. Here, each scenario is advanced as an ideal type to consider the relationship between norm and practice in productive ways. However, we can envision more scenarios and theory development to account for more varied dynamics.

For example, while scenario 3 highlights *how* change occurs when practices deviate from normative expectations, more work can be done to identify the spaces for agency and breaking points when disjunctures become so great as to intensify the pull to congruence – perhaps akin to a tipping point – that we hypothesize will eventually instantiate recognizable social change. One promising line of reasoning is already nascent in both constructivist and practice scholarship that views change as the result of dissonance between social structures and "agents' experience of who they are and what they do" (Flockhart 2016, 807). Flockhart and others (e.g., Steele 2005; Adler 2019) have zeroed in on responding to ontological insecurity as one possible mechanism that motivates change in response to such dissonance. They suggest that the motivation individuals have to maximize ontological security – that is, the "security of the self" which leads to us being "psychologically wired to prefer stability and consistency" and to pursue "self-esteem maximization" (Mitzen 2006, 341; Hopf 2010, 555; Flockhart 2016, 802–803, 806) – may provide the microfoundations for such a pull toward congruence. In other words, the drive for ontological security may force the disjunctures to the surface, motivating states (or other actors and sources of agency) to make practices coherent with a state's understanding of its values and principles in the form of the normative commitments it purports to uphold, in order to avoid shame or other states of ontological insecurity or psychological discomfort (Steele 2005; see also Laurence 2019, 18–19).

However, even if these microfoundations are at work, the acknowledged indeterminacy in the literature on how tensions between the "hardwired" preference for stability – which tends towards continuity – and the motivation to maximize ontological security and self-esteem in the face of dissonance will play out suggests more work is needed. In particular, our scenarios highlight that these agential or internal focused theoretical insights can more explicitly be linked to questions of when such pressures on either norms or practices may erupt into overt political conflict. As suggested by authors such as Bouris and Fernández-Molina (2024), disjunctures may remain resilient in path-dependent or cognitively or politically comfortable ways to avoid further undermining ontological security, or incongruence may be tolerated through some form of organized hypocrisy (Krasner 1999).

Similarly, the interaction of technological or other material forms of change, external shocks, or stochastic events – whether natural or social – as instigators of shifts in practices, akin to critical junctures, might be further investigated. As we noted in the Introduction, we are agnostic on the ultimate causes of change that might drive toward critical junctures, which we believe are myriad. Our framework is one way to identify patterns and processes of change that play out at such junctures, or even the construction of such junctures as "critical" when background conditions are shifting in an uncertain environment. Indeed, the relational ontology that our framework embraces resonates with the new scholarship on uncertainty in global politics (Katzenstein 2022; Matejova and Shesterinina 2023), while it also motivates further investigation into when uncertainty may give rise to transformational politics. This question is gaining increasing attention, especially in the face of potentially existential threats like climate change, AI, uncertain implications of biotechnology, polycrises or nuclear war which characterize the uncertain landscape of global politics that is motivating these analyses (Sears 2021; Lawrence et al. 2024; Bernstein 2024). Our framework suggests these threats alone cannot explain change, but rather change or transformation occurs in relation to the norm and practice dynamics we identify.

Beyond expanding our analytical approach, we see several areas where our scenarios could and should be put to use. First, our scenarios have been primarily applied to questions of state behaviour and global governance in this Element. As this conclusion has already highlighted, the scenarios can and should travel beyond this scope. For example, our scenarios could be adopted to consider broader questions of change in global politics regarding changing practices of sovereignty and shifting configurations of transnational authority, dynamics of empire and decolonization, and changing norms and practices around questions of human rights, race, and justice. Our scenarios could be also brought to conceptualize other ongoing changes within and across states and societies, as governments, firms, civil society groups, and other actors respond to challenges such as the rise of AI and its potential to disrupt established sectors of the economy from education to law to the arts. Finally, and more narrowly, our scenarios might bring analytic leverage to understanding changes in the relationships between and within CoPs in the context of states, organizations, private sector and transnational actors in global politics. Communities of practice – groups of agents united in a shared interest and utilizing common resources – are growing in analytical focus in IR, from government agencies, the halls of inter-state diplomacy, domestic and international organizations, firms and beyond, and ranging from communities of diplomats, humanitarian workers, peacekeepers, and feminist academics to overlapping intelligence and state security, private sector, and civil society communities of practice engaged in various practices of information gathering, and covert action while contesting norms of security, intelligence, warfare and privacy (e.g., Adler, Bremberg, and Sondarjee 2024; Laurence 2024b; Loleski 2024). Given the normative and practical foundations upon which such communities rest, being constrained by organizational and social principles and rules and engaged in practices of all kinds, our scenarios could be valuable in investigating the means by which CoP emerge, interact, and change in their thinking and behaviour, or not, over time.

In sum, we have aimed to provide new ways of seeing and analyzing the dynamics of social change in global politics. We believe our approach is widely applicable across fields and domains. In developing our framework, we have also contributed to conversations amongst two theoretical approaches within the field of IR that have been most engaged with questions of continuity of change. Given the current era is often characterized as one of increasingly rapid and uncertain change in the context of complex and even existential challenges, such conversations are needed now more than ever.

References

Abrahamsen, R., Andersen, L. R., & Sending, O. J. (2019). Introduction: Making liberal internationalism great again? *International Journal*, 74(1), 5–14.

Acharya, A. (2004). How ideas spread: Whose norms matter? Norm localization and institutional change in Asian regionalism. *International Organization*, 58(2), 239–275.

Acharya, A. (2014). *Constructing a Security Community in Southeast Asia ASEAN and the Problem of Regional Order*. New York: Routledge.

Adler, E. (2019). *World Ordering: A Social Theory of Cognitive Evolution*. Cambridge: Cambridge University Press.

Adler, E., Bremberg, N., & Sondarjee, M. (2024). Communities of practice in world politics: Advancing a research agenda. *Global Studies Quarterly*, 4(2), 1–13.

Adler, E. & Pouliot, V. (2011). International practices: Introduction and framework. In E. Adler and V. Pouliot, eds., *International Practices*. New York: Cambridge University Press, pp. 3–35.

Adler-Nissen, R. (2011). On a field trip with Bourdieu. *International Political Sociology*, 5(3), 327–330.

Adler-Nissen, R. (2014a). *Opting out of the European Union: Diplomacy, Sovereignty and European Integration*. Cambridge: Cambridge University Press.

Adler-Nissen, R. (2014b). Stigma management in International Relations: Transgressive identities, norms, and order in international society. *International Organization*, 68(1), 143–176.

Adler-Nissen, R. (2016). Towards a practice turn in EU studies: The everyday of European integration. *Journal of Common Market Studies*, 54(1), 87–103.

Adler-Nissen, R. (2024). The normalization of contestation: The sociology of knowledge and the challenges to the liberal international order. *Global Studies Quarterly*, 4(2), 1–5.

Adler-Nissen, R. & Pouliot, V. (2014). Power in practice: Negotiating the international intervention in Libya. *European Journal of International Relations*, 20(4), 889–911.

Archer, M. (1988). *Culture and Agency: The Place of Culture in Social Theory*. Cambridge: Cambridge University Press.

Bäckstrand, K. & Kylsäter, M. (2014). Old wine in new bottles? The legitimation and delegitimation of UN public–private partnerships for sustainable development from the Johannesburg Summit to the Rio+20 Summit. *Globalizations*, 11(3), 331–347.

Baer, D. B. (2022). The thaw on Russia's periphery has already started. *Foreign Policy*. https://foreignpolicy.com/2022/10/14/russia-ukraine-war-caucasus-georgia-armenia-azerbaijan-moldova-balkans-periphery-geopolitics-power-vacuum/.

Bartelson, J. (1995). *A Genealogy of Sovereignty*. Cambridge: Cambridge University Press.

Bennett, A. & Checkel, J. T., eds. (2014). *Process Tracing: From Metaphor to Analytic Tool*. Cambridge: Cambridge University Press.

Bernstein, S. (2001). *The Compromise of Liberal Environmentalism*. New York: Columbia University Press.

Bernstein, S. (2013). The Role and Place of a High-Level Political Forum in Strengthening the Global Institutional Framework for Sustainable Development. Commissioned by UNDESA [online]. https://sdgs.un.org/sites/default/files/documents/2331Bernstein%2520study%2520on%2520HLPF.pdf.

Bernstein, S. (2021). The assigning and erosion of responsibility for the global environment. In H. Hansen-Magnusson & A. Vetterlein, eds., *Handbook on Responsibility in International Relations*, New York: Routledge, pp. 139–152.

Bernstein, S. (2024). IR, climate politics, and change: Opportunities for productive engagement? *International Relations*, 38(3), 349–368.

Bernstein, S. and Brunnée, J. (2011). Consultants' Report on Options for Broader Reform of the Institutional Framework for Sustainable Development (IFSD): Structural, Legal, and Financial Aspects [online]. https://sdgs.un.org/publications/consultants-report-options-broader-reform-institutional-framework-sustainable#:~:text=This%20report%20assesses%20options%20for,on%20Sustainable%20Development%20(2002).

Bernstein, S. & Laurence, M. (2022). Practices and norms: Relationships, disjunctures and change. In A. Drieschova, C. Bueger, & T. Hopf, eds., *Conceptualizing International Practices*. New York: Cambridge University Press, pp. 77–99.

Betts, A. & Orchard, P. (2014). Introduction: The normative institutionalization-implementation gap. In A. Betts & P. Orchard, eds., *Implementation and World Politics: How International Norms Change Practice*. Oxford: Oxford University Press, pp. xviii–26.

Biersteker, T. J. & Weber, C. (1996). *State Sovereignty as Social Construct*. New York: Cambridge University Press.

Black, D. (2020). Development co-operation and the partnership–ownership nexus: Lessons from the Canada–Ghana experience. *Development Policy Review*, 38(S1), O112–O132.

Bode, I. (2024). Emergent normativity: Communities of practice, technology, and lethal autonomous weapons systems. *Global Studies Quarterly*, 4(1), 1–11.

Bode, I. & Huelss, H. (2018). Autonomous weapons systems and changing norms in international relations. *Review of International Studies*, 44(3), 393–413.

Bode, I. & Karlsrud, J. (2019). Implementation in practice: The use of force to protect civilians in United Nations peacekeeping. *European Journal of International Relations*, 25(2), 458–485. https://doi.org/10.1177/1354066118796540.

Bourdieu, P. (1977). *Outline of a Theory of Practice*. Cambridge: Cambridge University Press.

Bourbeau, P. (2017). The practice approach in global politics. *Journal of Global Security Studies*, 2(2), 170–182.

Bouris, D. & Fernández-Molina, I. (2024). The international norm–practice relationship, contested states, and the EU's territorial (un)differentiation toward Palestine and Western Sahara. *Global Studies Querterly* 4, 1–12.

Brosius, J. P. & Campbell, L. (2010). Collaborative event ethnography: Conservation and development trade-offs at the fourth world conservation congress. *Conservation and Society*, 8(4), 245–255.

Brown, S. (2020). The rise and fall of the aid effectiveness norm. *The European Journal of Development Research*, 32, 1230–1248.

Bueger, C. (2014). Pathways to practice: Praxiography and international politics. *European Political Science Review*, 6(3), 383–406.

Bueger, C. (2023). Document analysis: A praxiographic approach. In L. Maertens, L. R. Kimber, & F. Badache, eds., *International Organizations and Research Methods: An Introduction*. Ann Arbor: University of Michigan Press, pp. 151–157.

Bueger, C. & Gadinger, F. (2014). *International Practice Theory: New Perspectives*. New York: Palgrave Macmillan.

Bueger, C. & Gadinger, F. (2015). The play of international practice. *International Studies Quarterly*, 59(3), 449–460.

Bull, H. (1977). *The Anarchical Society: A Study of Order in World Politics*. London: Macmillan.

Bull, B. & McNeill, D. (2019). From market multilateralism to governance by goal setting: SDGs and the changing role of partnerships in a new global order. *Business and Politics*, 21(4), 464–486.

Burke, A. (2020). *Canada turning to foreign airlines to bring home citizens stranded by pandemic*. www.cbc.ca/news/politics/canada-repatrition-foreign-airlines-pandemic-covid-coronavirus-1.5557612.

Burrows, M. & Gnad, O. (2018). Between "Muddling Through" and "Grand Design": Regaining political initiative – The role of strategic foresight. *Futures*, 97, 6–17.

Busby, J. M. (2007). Bono made Jesse Helms cry: Jubilee 2000, debt relief, and moral action in international politics. *International Studies Quarterly*, 51(2), 247–275.

Buxton, N. (2019). *Multistakeholderism: A critical look*. Workshop Report. Corporate Power Project. Transnational Institute. www.tni.org/en/publication/multistakeholderism-a-critical-look.

Carbert, M. (2020). *Minister takes unconventional diplomatic steps to repatriate stranded Canadians amid COVID-19*, www.theglobeandmail.com/politics/article-minister-takes-unconventional-diplomatic-steps-to-repatriate-stranded/.

Carlsnaes, W. (1992). The agency-structure problem in foreign policy analysis. *International Studies Quarterly*, 36(3), 245–270.

CBC News. (2020). *Canada turning to foreign airlines to bring home citizens stranded by pandemic*, www.cbc.ca/news/politics/canada-repatrition-foreign-airlines-pandemic-covid-coronavirus-1.5557612.

Chayes, A., & Chayes, A. H. (1993). On compliance. *International Organization*, 47(2), 175–205.

Checkel, J. T. (1998). The constructivist turn in International Relations theory. *World Politics*, 50(2), 324–348.

Checkel, J. T. (2005). International institutions and socialization in Europe: Introduction and framework. *International Organization*, 59(4), 801–882.

Chelotti, N., Dasandi, N., & Mikhaylov, S. J. (2022). Do intergovernmental organizations have a socialization effect on member state preferences? Evidence from the UN general debate. *International Studies Quarterly*, 66(1), 1–17.

Clarke, P. (2003). Building a global partnership for development? In R. Black & H. White, eds., *Targeting Development: Critical Perspectives on the Millennium Development Goals*. New York: Routledge, pp. 307–322.

Coe, B. N. (2019). *Sovereignty in the South: Intrusive Regionalism in Africa, Latin America, and Southeast Asia*. Cambridge: Cambridge University Press.

Cohen, R. (2023). *War in Ukraine has changed Europe forever*, New York Times. www.nytimes.com/2023/02/26/world/europe/ukraine-russia-war.html.

Commission on International Development (Pearson Commission). (1969). *Partners in Development*, https://unesdoc.unesco.org/ark:/48223/pf0000206935.

Cook, L. (2023). *NATO to hold Ukraine meeting despite Hungary's objections*, Associatated Press. https://apnews.com/article/nato-hungary-ukraine-rights-minorities-3b6581af80d5d51d511ac666eeef9288.

Cooper, A. F. & Cornut, J. (2019). The changing practices of frontline diplomacy: New directions for inquiry. *Review of International Studies*, 45(2), 300–319.

Cornut, J. (2018). Diplomacy, agency, and the logic of improvisation and virtuosity in practice. *European Journal of International Relations*, 24(3), 712–736.

Cornut, J. & Zamaróczy, N. (2020). How can documents speak about practices? Practice tracing, the Wikileaks cables, and diplomatic culture. *Cooperation and Conflict*, 56(3), 328–345.

Crosbie, W. (2018). A consular code to supplement the VCCR. *The Hague Journal of Diplomacy*, 13(2), 233–243.

Czarniawska, B. (2009). Emerging institutions: Pyramids or anthills? *Organization Studies*, 30(4), 423–441.

Davies, M. (2016). A community of practice: Explaining change and continuity in ASEAN's diplomatic environment. *The Pacific Review*, 29(2), 211–233.

Davis, C. (2010). NATO's next strategic concept: How the alliance's new strategy will reshape global security. *Strategic Studies Quarterly*, 4(4), 32–49.

De Luce, D. (2020). *The pandemic shows WHO lacks authority to force governments to divulge information, experts say*, www.nbcnews.com/health/health-news/pandemic-shows-who-lacks-authority-force-governments-divulge-information-experts-n1203046.

Deitelhoff, N. & Zimmermann, L. (2019). Norms under challenge: Unpacking the dynamics of norm robustness. *Journal of Global Security Studies*, 4(1), 2–17.

Doty, R. L. (1997). Aporia: A critical exploration of the agent-structure problematique in international relations theory. *European Journal of International Relations*, 3(3), 365–392.

Drieschova, A., Bueger, C., & Hopf, T., eds. (2022). *Conceptualizing International Practices: Directions for the Practice Turn in International Relations*. Cambridge: Cambridge University Press.

Duvall, R. & Chowdhury, A. (2011). Practices of theory. In E. Adler & V. Pouliot, eds., *International Practices*. Cambridge: Cambridge University Press, pp. 335–354.

Eggeling, K. A. & Adler-Nissen, R. (2021). The show must go on(line): The synthetic situation in diplomacy. *Global Studies Quarterly*, 1(2), 1–32.

Elzas, S. (2020). *France organises flights, transport for 30,000 citizens still stranded abroad*, www.rfi.fr/en/international/20200327-france-organises-transport-for-30-000-citizens-still-stranded-abroad-coronavirus-lockdown-grounded-flights-covid19.

Emirbayer, M. (1997). Manifesto for a relational sociology. *American Journal of Sociology*, 103(2), 281–317.

Epstein, C. (2008). *The Power of Words in International Relations: Birth of an Anti-Whaling Discourse*. Cambridge, MA: MIT Press.

Erlanger, S. (2022). Fear of Russia Brings New Purpose and Unity to NATO, Once Again, *New York Times*. January 14. www.nytimes.com/2022/01/14/world/europe/nato-russia-ukraine-europe.html.

European Parliament. (2020). *Repatriation of EU citizens during the COVID-19 crisis: The role of the EU Civil Protection Mechanism*, www.europarl.europa.eu/RegData/etudes/BRIE/2020/649359/EPRS_BRI(2020)649359_EN.pdf.

European Peacebuilding Liaison Office. (2017). *The Lisbon Reform Treaty and Its effects on CFSP/CSDP*, https://eplo.org/wp-content/uploads/2017/03/EPLO_Lisbon_Reform_Treaty_and_its_Effect_on_CFSP.pdf.

European Union. (1992). *Treaty on European Union*, https://eur-lex.europa.eu/legal-content/EN/TXT/?uri=CELEX:11992M/TXT.

Farge, E. (2023). *How the World Health Organization could fight future pandemics*, www.reuters.com/business/healthcare-pharmaceuticals/how-world-health-organization-could-fight-future-pandemics-2023-05-23/.

Faviero G. F., Stocking B. M., Hoffman S. J., et al. (2022). An effective pandemic treaty requires accountability. *The Lancet Public Health*, 7(9), e730–e731.

Fazal, T. M. (2022). The return of conquest. *Foreign Affairs*, May/June 2022. https://www.foreignaffairs.com/articles/ukraine/2022-04-06/ukraine-russia-war-return-conquest.

Finnemore, M. (1996). *National Interests in International Society*. Ithaca: Cornell University Press.

Finnemore, M. (2003). *The Purpose of Intervention: Changing Beliefs about the Use of Force*. Ithaca: Cornell University Press.

Finnemore, M. & Sikkink, K. (1998). International norm dynamics and political change. *International Organization*, 52(4), 887–917.

Finnemore, M. & Sikkink, K. (2001). Taking stock: The constructivist research program in International Relations and Comparative Politics. *Annual Review of Political Science*, 4(1), 391–416.

Fioretos, O. (2011). Historical institutionalism in International Relations. *International Organization*, 65(1), 367–399.

Flockhart, T. (2016). The problem of change in constructivist theory: Ontological security seeking and agent motivation. *Review of International Studies*, 42(5), 799–820.

Flockhart, T. (2022). Theorizing change in the English school. In T. Flockhart & Z. Paikin, eds., *Rebooting Global International Society: Change, Contestation and Resilience*. Cham: Palgrave Macmillan, pp. 21–39.

Florini, A. (1996). The evolution of international norms. *International Studies Quarterly*, 40(3), 363–389.

Foreign Affairs Committee. (2020) *Flying Home: The FCO's Consular Response to the COVID-19 Pandemic*. https://publications.parliament.uk/pa/cm5801/cmselect/cmfaff/643/64305.htm.

France 24. (2024). Macron again declines to rule out Western ground operations in Ukraine "at some point". March 16. www.france24.com/en/europe/20240316-macron-says-western-ground-operations-ukraine-necessary-some-point.

Fukuda-Parr, S. & Muchhala, B. (2020). The southern origins of sustainable development goals: Ideas, actors, aspirations. *World Development*, 126 (104706), 1–11.

Gadinger F. (2022). The normativity of international practices. In A. Drieschova, C. Bueger, & T. Hopf, eds., *Conceptualizing International Practices: Directions for the Practice Turn in International Relations*. Cambridge: Cambridge University Press, pp. 100–121.

Gilpin, R. (1981). *War and Change in World Politics*, Cambridge: Cambridge University Press.

Glas, A. (2022). *Practicing Peace: Conflict Management in Southeast Asia and South America*, Oxford: Oxford University Press.

Glas, A. & Balogun, E. (2020). Norms in practice: People-centric governance in ASEAN and ECOWAS. *International Affairs*, 96(4), 1015–1032.

Glas, A. & Laurence, M. (2022). Changing norms in practice: Noninterference in the UN and ASEAN. *Journal of Global Security Studies*, 7(2), 1–17.

Glas, A. & Martel, S. (2024). Boundary work, overlapping identities, and liminality in communities of practice: Diplomacy in ASEAN and beyond. *Global Studies Quarterly*, 4(1), 1–11.

Glas, A., van der Linden, C., Hoffmann, M. J., & Denemark, R. (2018). Understanding multilateral treaty-making as constitutive practice. *Journal of Global Security Studies*, 3(3), 339–357.

Goddard, S., Krebs, R., Kreuder-Sonnen, C., & Rittberger, B. (2024). Contestation of Liberal World Orders. *Global Studies Quarterly*, 4(2), 1–12.

Goldstein, M. (2020). *US State Department Brings Home over 85,000 Americans in Coronavirus Crisis*, www.forbes.com/sites/michaelgoldstein/2020/04/10/us-state-department-brings-home-more-than-50000-americans-in-coronavirus-crisis/?sh=4aed51e55d93.

Government of Australia. (2022). *Consular Services Charter*, www.smartraveller.gov.au/consular-services/consular-services-charter.

Government of Canada. (2016). *Canadian Consular Services Charter*. https://travel.gc.ca/assistance/emergency-info/consular/canadian-consular-services-charter.

Government of Canada. (2021). *Transcript – Episode 49: A chat with Brent Robson on the Canadian COVID-19 repatriation operation*, www.international.gc.ca/gac-amc/podcasts-transcript-balados-transcription-ep49.aspx?lang=eng.

Government of Canada. (2022). *If You're Abroad, It's Time for You to Come Home*, www.international.gc.ca/world-monde/stories-histoires/2021/covid-repatriation-covid-rapatriement.aspx?lang=eng.

Government of Canada. (2023). *About Consular Services*, https://travel.gc.ca/assistance/emergency-info/consular.

Government of Estonia. (2015). *Estonia's Constitution of 1992 with Amendments through 2015*, www.constituteproject.org/constitution/Estonia_2015.pdf?lang=en.

Government of Germany. (1974). *Law on consular officers, their functions and powers (Consular Law)*, www.auswaertiges-amt.de/blob/232092/835fd523b3d0de7a3e13bd6a851da1b7/konsulargesetz-data.pdf.

Government of the United Kingdom. (2020). *Flying Home: The FCO's consular response to the COVID-19 pandemic: Government Response to the Committee's Third Report*, https://publications.parliament.uk/pa/cm5801/cmselect/cmfaff/859/85902.htm.

Government of the United Kingdom. (2022). *Support for British Nationals Abroad*, www.gov.uk/government/collections/support-for-british-nationals-abroad.

Government of the United States of America. (2021). *COVID-19: State carried out historic repatriation effort but should strengthen its preparedness for future crises*, www.gao.gov/products/gao-22-104354.

Graeger, N. & Lindgren, W. Y. (2018). The duty of care for citizens abroad: Security and responsibility in the In Amenas and Fukushima crises. *The Hague Journal of Diplomacy*, 13(2), 188–210.

Graham-Harrison, E., Beaumont, P., Harding, L., Sauer, P., & Henley, J. (2022). *Airstrikes at dawn as Russia begins "war of aggression" with Ukraine*, www

.theguardian.com/world/2022/feb/24/airstrikes-dawn-russia-begins-war-aggression-with-ukraine-vladimir-putin.

G77 and China. (2015). *Ministerial Declaration*, www.g77.org/doc/Declaration2015.htm.

Hannon, E., Hanbali, L., Lehtimaki S., & Schwalbe, N. (2022). Why we still need a pandemic treaty. *The Lancet Global Health*, 10(9), E1232–E1233.

Hathaway, O. & Philips-Robins, A. (2020). *COVID-19 and international law series: WHO's pandemic response and the International Health Regulations*, www.justsecurity.org/73753/covid-19-and-international-law-series-whos-pandemic-response-and-the-international-health-regulations/.

He, K. & Feng, H. (2015). Transcending rationalism and constructivism: Chinese leaders' operational codes, socialization processes, and multilateralism after the Cold War. *European Political Science Review*, 7(3), 401–426. https://doi.org/10.1017/S1755773914000241.

Hedling, E. & Bremberg, N. (2021). Practice approaches to the digital transformations of diplomacy: Toward a new research agenda. *International Studies Review*, 23(4), 1595–1618.

Helleiner, E. (2019). The life and times of embedded liberalism: Legacies and innovations since Bretton Woods. *Review of International Political Economy*, 26(6), 1112–1135. https://doi.org/10.1080/09692290.2019.1607767.

Higham, I., Bäckstrand, K., Fritzsche, F., & Koliev, F. (2024). Multistakeholder partnerships for sustainable development: Promises and pitfalls. *Annual Review of Environment and Resources* 49 (Review in Advance), www-annualreviews-org.myaccess.library.utoronto.ca/content/journals/10.1146/annurev-environ-051823-115857.

Hoorens, S., Nederveen, F., Niemi, T., et al. (2019). *Consular Services to Citizens Abroad: Insights from an International Comparative Study*, www.rand.org/pubs/research_reports/RR4288.html.

Hopf, T. (2002). *Social Construction of Foreign Policy: Identities and Foreign Policies, Moscow, 1955 and 1999*. Ithaca: Cornell Unvieristy Press.

Hopf, T. (2010). The logic of habit in International Relations. *European Journal of International Relations*, 16(4), 539–561.

Hopf, T. (2011). International Security in Practice: The Politics of NATO–Russia Diplomacy. By Vincent Pouliot. New York: Cambridge University Press, 2010. 306p. $85.00 cloth, $30.00 paper. *Perspectives on Politics*, 9(3), 772–773.

Hopf, T. (2018). Change in international practices. *European Journal of International Relations*, 24(3), 687–711.

Ikenberry, J. G. (2018). The end of the liberal international order? *International Affairs*, 94(1), 7–23.

International Commission on Intervention and State Sovereignty. (2001). *The responsibility to protect: Report of the International Commission on Intervention and State Sovereignty*, https://idl-bnc-idrc.dspacedirect.org/bitstream/handle/10625/18432/IDL-18432.pdf?sequence=6&isAllowed=y.

Jackson, P. (2009). Pierre Bourdieu. In J. Edkins & N. Vaughan-Williams, eds., *Critical Theorists and International Relations*. New York: Routledge, pp. 102–113.

Jackson, H. (2020). *Canada will not be doing another repatriation amid coronavirus pandemic: Champagne*, https://globalnews.ca/news/7479769/canada-no-coronavirus-repatriation/.

Johnston, A. I. (2001). Treating international institutions as social environments. *International Studies Quarterly*, 45(4), 487–515.

Jurkovich, M. (2020). What isn't a norm? Redefining the conceptual boundaries of "norms" in the human rights literature. *International Studies Review*, 22(3), 693–711.

Jütersonke, O., Kobayashi, K., Krause, K., & Yuan, X. (2021). Norm contestation and normative transformation in global peacebuilding order(s): The cases of China, Japan, and Russia. *International Studies Quarterly*, 65(4), 944–959.

Katz, R. & Fischer, J. (2010). The revised international health regulations: A framework for global pandemic response. *Global Health Governance*, 3(2), 1–18.

Katzenstein, P. (1996). Introduction: Alternative perspectives on national security. In P. Katzenstein, ed., *The Culture of National Security: Norms and Identity in World Politics*. New York: Columbia University Press, pp. 33–72.

Katzenstein, P. (ed.) (2022). *Uncertainty and Its Discontents: Worldviews in World Politics*. Cambridge: Cambridge University Press.

Kobayashi, K., Krause, K., & Yuan, X. (2022). Pathways to socialisation: China, Russia, and competitive norm socialisation in a changing global order. *Review of International Studies*, 48(3), 560–582. https://doi.org/10.1017/S0260210522000146.

Keck, M. E. & Sikkink, K. (1998). *Activists beyond Borders: Advocacy Networks in International Politics*. Ithaca: Cornell University Press.

Kirshner, J. (2024). Classical realism and the challenge of global economic governance. *Oxford Review of Economic Policy*, 40(2), 246–255. https://doi.org/10.1093/oxrep/grae010.

Kornprobst, M. & Strobl, S. (2021). Global health: An order struggling to keep up with globalization. *International Affairs*, 97(5), 1541–1558.

Kramarz, T. (2020). *Forgotten Values: The World Bank and Environmental Partnerships*. Cambridge, MA: MIT Press.

Krasner, S. (1999). *Sovereignty: Organized Hypocrisy*. Princeton: Princeton University Press.

Kreuder-Sonnen, C. & Zürn, M. (2020). After fragmentation: Norm collisions, interface conflicts, and conflict management. *Global Constitutionalism*, 9(2), 241–267.

Krook, M. L. & True, J. (2010). Rethinking the life cycles of international norms: The United Nations and the global promotion of gender equality. *European Journal of International Relations*, 18(1), 103–127.

Kurki, M., (2022). Relational revolution and relationality in IR: New conversations. *Review of International Studies*, 48(5), 821–836.

Lake, D. A., Martin, L. L., & Risse, T. (2021). Challenges to the liberal order: Reflections on international organization. *International Organization*, 75(2), 225–257.

Laurence, M. (2019). An "impartial" force? Normative ambiguity and practice change in UN peace operations. *International Peacekeeping*, 26(3), 256–280.

Laurence, M. (2024a). Interpretive agency, change, and the role of individuals in UN peace operations. *International Peacekeeping* Online First, 1–24.

Laurence, M. (2024b). *Intrusive Impartiality: Learning, Contestation, and Practice Change in United Nations Peace Operations*. New York: Oxford University Press.

Lave, J. & Wenger, E. (1991). *Situated Learning: Legitimate Peripheral Participation*. New York: Cambridge University Press.

Lawrence, M., Homer-Dixon, T., Janzwood, S., et al. (2024). Global polycrisis: The causal mechanisms of crisis entanglement. *Global Sustainability*, 7(e6), 1–16.

Lesch, M. & Loh, D. (2022). Field overlaps, normativity, and the contestation of practices in China's Belt and Road Initiative. *Global Studies Quarterly*, 2(4), 1–12.

Lloyd-Sherlock, P., Sempe, L., McKee, M., & Guntupalli, A. (2021). Problems of data availability and quality for COVID-19 and older people in low- and middle-income countries. *The Gerontologist*, 61(2), 141–144.

Loh, D. M. H. (2020). Institutional habitus, state identity, and China's Ministry of Foreign Affairs. *International Studies Review*, 22(4), 879–902.

Loh, D. M. H. (2024). *China's Rising Foreign Ministry: Practices and Representations of Assertive Diplomacy*. Stanford, CA: Stanford University Press.

Loleski, S. (2024). *Unleashing and Restraining American Cyber Power: Affordances, Informational Imaginaries, and U.S. Offensive Practices*. PhD Thesis, University of Toronto.

Long, G., Clough, E., & Rietig, K. (2022). Global partnerships for the SDGs. In E. Murphy, A. Banerjee, & P. P. Walsh, eds., *Partnerships and the*

Sustainable Development Goals. Cham: Springer Nature, pp. 27–39. https://doi.org/10.1007/978-3-031-07461-5_3.

Lucero-Prisno, D. E. III, Essar, M.Y., Ahmadi, A., Lin, X., & Adebayo, Y. (2020). Conflict and COVID-19: A double burden for Afghanistan's healthcare system. *Conflict and Health*, 14(65), 1–3.

Mallapaty, S. (2022). *Genome data gaps could stymie search for new COVID variant*, www.nature.com/articles/d41586-022-00894-x.

Manahan, M. & Kumar, M. (2021). *The Great Takeover: Mapping of Multistakeholderism in Global Governance*. Transnational Institute, www.tni.org/en/publication/the-great-takeover.

Mansfield, E. D. & Rudra, N. (2021). Embedded liberalism in the digital era. *International Organization*, 75(2), 558–585.

March, J. G. & Olsen, J. P. (1998). The institutional dynamics of international political orders. *International Organization*, 52(4), 943–969.

Marion Suiseeya, K. R. & Zanotti, L. (2019). Making influence visible: Innovating ethnography at the Paris Climate Summit. *Global Environmental Politics*, 19(2), 38–60.

Matejova, M. & Shesterinina, A., eds. (2023). *Uncertainty in Global Politics*. London: Routledge.

May, K. (2020). *Coming Home: Global Affairs' Quest to Repatriate Canadians*, https://ppforum.ca/publications/coming-home-global-affairs-quest-to-repatriate-canadians/.

McCourt, D. M. (2016). Practice theory and relationalism as the new constructivism. *International Studies Quarterly*, 60(3), 475–485.

McNamara, K. R. & Newman, A. L. (2020). The big reveal: COVID-19 and globalization's great transformations. *International Organization*, 74(S1), E59–E77. https://doi.org/10.1017/S0020818320000387.

Mearsheimer, J. J. (2019). Bound to fail: The rise and fall of the Liberal International Order. *International Security*, 43(4), 7–50.

Meister, S. (2022). *A paradigm shift: EU-Russia relations after the war in Ukraine*, https://carnegieeurope.eu/2022/11/29/paradigm-shift-eu-russia-relations-after-war-in-ukraine-pub-88476.

Mitzen, J. (2006). Ontological security in world politics: State identity and the security dilemma. *European Journal of International Relations*, 12(3), 341–370.

Nair, D. (2019). Saving face in diplomacy: A political sociology of face-to-face interactions in the Association of Southeast Asian Nations. *European Journal of International Relations*, 25(3), 672–697.

Nair, D. (2020). Sociability in international politics: Golf and ASEAN's cold war diplomacy. *International Political Sociology*, 14(2), 196–214.

Neumann, I. B. (2002). Returning practice to the linguistic turn: The case of diplomacy. *Millennium*, 31(3), 627–651.

Newell, P., Srivastava, S., Naess, L. O., et al. (2021). Toward transformative climate justice: An emerging research agenda. *WIREs Climate Change*, 12(6), e733.

North Atlantic Treaty Organization. (2023a). *Collective defence and article 5*, www.nato.int/cps/en/natohq/topics_110496.htm#:~:text=Article%205%20provides%20that%20if,to%20assist%20the%20Ally%20attacked.

North Atlantic Treaty Organization. (2023b). *Enlargement and article 10*, www.nato.int/cps/en/natohq/topics_49212.htm.

OECD. (n.d.a). *Grants by Private Agenceies and NGOs*, www.oecd.org/en/data/indicators/grants-by-private-agencies-and-ngos.

OECD. (n.d.b). *ODA Trends and Statistics*, www.oecd.org/en/topics/oda-trends-and-statistics.html.

Office of the President of Russia. (2022). *Address by the President of the Russian Federation*, http://en.kremlin.ru/events/president/news/67843.

Okano-Heijmans, M. (2010). *Change in Consular Assistance and the Emergence of Consular Diplomacy*. The Hague: Netherlands Institute of International Relations. https://www.clingendael.org/publication/change-consular-assistance-and-emergence-consular-diplomacy.

Oksamytna, K. & Wilén, N. (2022). Adoption, adaptation or chance? Inter-organisational diffusion of the protection of civilians norm from the UN to the African Union. *Third World Quarterly*, 43(10), 2357–2374.

Orchard, P. & Wiener, A. (2024). Norm research in theory and practice. In P. Orchard & A. Wiener, eds., *Contesting the World: Norm Research in Theory and Practice*. Cambridge: Cambridge University Press, pp. 1–28.

Osnos, E. (2022). *What is China learning from Russia's invasion of Ukraine?* www.newyorker.com/news/daily-comment/what-is-china-learning-from-russias-invasion-of-ukraine.

Panke, D. & Petersohn, U. (2012). Why international norms disappear sometimes. *European Journal of International Relations*, 18(4), 719–742.

Pedersen-Macnab, M. & Bernstein, S. (2024). When socialization fails: Breaking the habit of engagement with China. *International Affairs*, 100(5), 2113–2132. https://doi.org/10.1093/ia/iiae114.

Percy, S. V. & Sandholtz, W. (2022). Why norms rarely die. *European Journal of International Relations*, 28(4), 934–954.

Petersmann, E. (2020). Economic disintegration? Political, economic, and legal drivers and the need for "greening embedded trade liberalism." *Journal of International Economic Law*, 23(2), 347–370. https://doi.org/10.1093/jiel/jgaa005.

Pierson, P. (2000). Increasing returns, path dependence, and the study of politics. *The American Political Science Review*, 94(2), 251–267.

Pouliot, V. (2008). The logic of practicality: A theory of practice of security communities. *International Organization*, 62(2), 257–288.

Pouliot, V. (2010). *International Security in Practice: The Politics of NATO-Russia Diplomacy*. Cambridge: Cambridge University Press.

Pouliot, V. (2014). Practice tracing. In A. Bennett, & J. T. Checkel, eds., *Process Tracing: From Metaphor to Analytic Tool*. Strategies for Social Inquiry. Cambridge: Cambridge University Press, pp. 237–259.

Pouliot, V. (2016). Hierarchy in practice: Multilateral diplomacy and the governance of international security. *European Journal of International Security*, 1(1), 5–26.

Pouliot, V. (2020). Historical institutionalism meets practice theory: Renewing the selection process of the United Nations Secretary-General. *International Organization*, 74(4), 742–772.

Pouliot, V. (2021). The grey area of institutional change: How the Security Council transforms its practices on the fly. *Journal of Global Security Studies*, 6(30), 1–18.

Pouliot, V. & Thérien, J. P. (2018). Global governance: A struggle over universal values. *International Studies Review*, 20(1), 55–73.

Pratt, S. (2020). From norms to normative configurations: A pragmatist and relational approach to theorizing normativity in IR. *International Theory*, 12(1), 59–82.

Pratt, S. F. (2022). *Normative Transformation and the War on Terrorism: The Evolution of Targeted Killing, Torture, and Private Military Contractingss*. Cambridge: Cambridge University Press.

Pu, X. (2012). Socialisation as a two-way process: Emerging powers and the diffusion of international norms. *The Chinese Journal of International Politics*, 5(4), 341–367.

Pullen, R. K. & Frost, C. (2022). *Putin's Ukraine invasion: Do declarations of war still exist?* https://theconversation.com/putins-ukraine-invasion-do-declarations-of-war-still-exist-177880.

Raymond, M. & DeNardis, L. (2015). Multistakeholderism: Anatomy of an inchoate global institution. *International Theory*, 7(3), 572–616.

Reinsberg, B. & Westerwinter, O. (2021). The global governance of international development: Documenting the rise of multi-stakeholder partnerships and identifying underlying theoretical explanations. *Review of International Organizations*, 16(1), 59–94.

Rösch, F. (2020). Affect, practice, and change: Dancing world politics at the Congress of Vienna. *Cooperation and Conflict*, 56(2), 123–140.

Rosenberg, A. S. (2022). *Undesirable Immigrants: Why Racism Persists in International Migration*. Princeton: Princeton University Press.

Rouse, J. (2001). Two concepts of practices. In T. R. Schatzki, K. K. Cetina, & E. von Savigny, eds., *The Practice Turn in Contemporary Theory*. London: Routledge, pp. 198–208.

Roy-Chaudhury, S. (2023). *The Ukraine war and an emboldened China on the LAC*, https://thediplomat.com/2023/04/the-ukraine-war-and-an-emboldened-china-on-the-lac/.

Ruggie, J. G. (1982). International regimes, transactions, and change: Embedded liberalism in the postwar economic order. *International Organization*, 36(2), 379–415.

Ruggie, J. G. (1997). Globalization and the Embedded Liberal Compromise: The End of an Era? (Working Paper No. MPIfG 97/1). Köln: Max Planck Institute for the Study of Societies.

Ruggie, J. G. (1998). *Constructing the World Polity*. London: Routledge.

Ruggie, J. G. (2007). Global markets and global governance the prospects for convergence. In S. Bernstein & L. Pauly, eds., *Global Liberalism and Political Order: Toward a New Grand Compromise?* Albany: State University of New York Press, pp. 23–48.

Sandholtz, W. (2008). Dynamics of international norm change: Rules against wartime plunder. *European Journal of International Relations*, 14(1), 101–131.

Schatz, E. (2009). Ethnographic immersion and the study of politics. In E. Schatz, ed., *Political Ethnography: What Immersion Contributes to the Study of Power*. Chicago: University of Chicago Press, pp. 1–22.

Schatzki, T. R. (2001). Introduction: Practice theory. In T. R. Schatzki, K. K. Cetina, & E. von Savigny, eds., *The Practice Turn in Contemporary Theory*. New York: Routledge, pp. 10–23.

Schindler, S. & Wille, T. (2015). Change in and through practice: Pierre Bourdieu, Vincent Pouliot, and the end of the Cold War. *International Theory*, 7(2), 330–359.

Schmidt, S. (2014). Foreign military presence and the changing practice of sovereignty: A pragmatist explanation of norm change. *The American Political Science Review*, 108(4), 817–829.

Scholz, O. (2023). *The global Zeitenwende: How to avoid a new Cold War in a multipolar era*, www.foreignaffairs.com/germany/olaf-scholz-global-zeitenwende-how-avoid-new-cold-war.

Searle, J. (1995). *The Construction of Social Reality*. New York: Free Press.

Sears, N. (2021). International politics in the age of existential threats. *Journal of Global Security Studies* 6(3, September), 1–23.

Sending, O. J., Pouliot, V., & Neumann I. B. (2011). The future of diplomacy: Changing practices, evolving relationships. *International Journal*, 66(3), 527–542.

Serey, R., Bivens, R. T., & Glas, A. (2024). "This is not the 90s": Myanmar and change in ASEAN's normative order. *Pacific Affairs*, 97(4), 773–794.

Simmons, B. A. (2009). *Mobilizing for Human Rights: International Law in Domestic Politics*. Cambridge: Cambridge University Press.

Sjursen, H. (2005). Understanding the common foreign and security policy: Analytical building blocks. In M. Knodt & S. Princen, eds., *Understanding the European Union's External Relations*. New York: Routledge, pp. 34–52.

Sondermann, E., & Ulbert, C. (2021). Transformation through "meaningful" partnership? SDG 17 as metagovernance norm and its global health implementation. *Politics and Governance*, 9(1), 152–163.

Spruyt, H. (1994). Institutional Selection in International-Relations – State Anarchy as Order. *International Organization*, 48(3), 527–557.

Standfield, C. (2020). Gendering the practice turn in diplomacy. *European Journal of International Relations*, 26(1_suppl), 140–165.

The Standing Senate Committee on Foreign Affairs and International Trade. (2007). *The ation of Canadians from Lebanon in July 2006: Implications for the Government of Canada*, https://sencanada.ca/content/sen/Committee/391/fore/rep/rep12may07-e.pdf.

Steele, B. J. (2005). Ontological security and the power of self-identity: British neutrality and the American Civil War. *Review of International Studies*, 31(3), 519–540.

Stein, J. G. (2011). Background knowledge in the foreground: Conversations about competent practice in "sacred space." In: Adler E, Pouliot V, eds. *International Practices*. Cambridge Studies in International Relations. Cambridge: Cambridge University Press, pp. 87–107.

Stibbe, D. & Prescott, D. (2020). *The Partnership Guidebook: A practical guide to building high-impact multi-stakeholder partnerships for the Sustainable Development Goals*. The Partnering Initiative and UNDESA.

Stimmer, A. & Wisken, L. (2019). The dynamics of dissent: When actions are louder than words. *International Affairs*, 95(3), 515–533.

Taggart, J. R. (2022). Global development governance in the "interregnum." *Review of International Political Economy*, 29(3), 904–927.

Taggart, J. R. & Abraham, K. V. (2024). Norm dynamics in a post-hegemonic world: Multistakeholder global governance and the end of liberal international order. *Review of International Political Economy*, 31(1), 354–381.

Taylor, L. (2023). COVID-19: WHO treaty on future pandemics is being watered down, warn health leaders. *British Medical Journal*, 381(1246), 1–2.

Terhalle, M. (2012). Reciprocal socialization: Rising powers and the west. *International Studies Perspectives*, 12(4), 341–361.

Thelen, K. & Steinmo, S. (1992). Historic Institutionalism in Comparative Politics. In S. Steinmo, K. Thelen, & F. Longsreth, eds., *Structuring Politics: Historical Institutionalism in Comparative Analysis*. Cambridge: Cambridge University Press, pp. 1–32.

Thérien, J. P. & Pouliot, V. (2020). Global governance as patchwork: The making of the sustainable development goals. *Review of International Political Economy*, 27(3), 612–636.

Troszczynska-van Genderen, W. (2015). *The Lisbon Treaty's Provisions on CFSP/CSDP State of Implementation*, www.europarl.europa.eu/RegData/etudes/IDAN/2015/570446/EXPO_IDA(2015)570446_EN.pdf.

True, J. & Wiener, A. (2019). Everyone wants (a) peace: The dynamics of rhetoric and practice on "Women, Peace and Security." *International Affairs*, 95(3), 553–574.

UNGA. (2015). *Transforming Our World: The 2030 Agenda for Sustainable Development*. A/RES/70/1. https://sdgs.un.org/publications/transforming-our-world-2030-agenda-sustainable-development-17981.

United Nations. (1963). *Vienna convention on consular relations*, https://legal.un.org/ilc/texts/instruments/english/conventions/9_2_1963.pdf.

United Nations. (1992). *Report of the United Nations Conference on Environment and Development: Rio Declration on Environment and Development*, www.un.org/esa/dsd/agenda21/Agenda%2021.pdf.

United Nations. (2002). *Report of the World Summit on Sustainable Development, Johannesburg, South Africa*, https://digitallibrary.un.org/record/478154?ln=en.

United Nations. (2003). *Monterrey Consensus of the International Conference on Financing for Development*, www.un.org/en/development/desa/population/migration/generalassembly/docs/globalcompact/A_CONF.198_11.pdf.

United Nations. (2013). *A renewed global partnership for development. A report of the UN System Task Team on the Post-2015 UN Development Agenda*, www.un.org/en/development/desa/policy/untaskteam_undf/glob_dev_rep_2013.pdf.

United Nations. (2015). *Transforming our world: The 2030 agenda for sustainable development*, https://sdgs.un.org/2030agenda.

United Nations. (2021a). *Millennium Development Goals indicators*, http://mdgs.un.org/unsd/mdg/Host.aspx?Content=Indicators/OfficialList.htm.

United Nations. (2021b). *Sustainable Development Goals partnership platform*, https://sustainabledevelopment.un.org/partnerships/.

United Nations. (n.d.). *International human rights law*, www.ohchr.org/en/professionalinterest/pages/internationallaw.aspx.

University of Rochester News Center. (2022). *Fact-checking Putin's claims that Ukraine and Russia are "one people,"* www.rochester.edu/newscenter/ukraine-history-fact-checking-putin-513812/.

Van Beusekomo, M. (2021). *Study: US COVID cases, deaths far higher than reported*, www.cidrap.umn.edu/news-perspective/2021/01/study-us-covid-cases-deaths-far-higher-reported.

Weber, W. (2020). The normative grammar of relational analysis: Recognition theory's contribution to understanding short-comings in IR's relational turn. *International Studies Quarterly*, 64(3), 641–648.

Wendt, A. (1992). Anarchy is what states make of it: The social construction of power politics. *International Organization*, 46(2), 391–425.

Wiener, A. (2004). Contested compliance: Interventions on the normative structure of world politics. *European Journal of International Relations*, 10(2), 189–234.

Wiener, A. (2009). Enacting meaning-in-use: Qualitative research on norms and international relations. *Review of International Studies*, 35(1), 175–193.

Wiener, A. (2018). *Constitution of Norms in Global International Relations*. Cambridge: Cambridge University Press.

World Commission on Environment and Development (WCED), (1987). *Our Common Future*. Oxford: Oxford University Press.

World Health Organization (n.d.). *The global health observatory – health emergencies*, www.who.int/data/gho/data/major-themes/health-emergencies/GHO/health-emergencies.

World Health Organization. (2005). *International health regulations (2005)*, www.who.int/health-topics/international-health-regulations#tab=tab_1.

World Health Organization. (2019). *Activity report 2018–2019: Support to countries for strengthening public health capacities required under the International health regulations* (2005), https://apps.who.int/iris/handle/10665/333792.

World Health Organization. (2021a). *Two decades dedicated to capacity building for health emergency preparedness and response*, www.who.int/news/item/10-12-2021-two-decades-dedicated-to-capacity-building-for-health-emergency-preparedness-and-response.

World Health Organization. (2021b). *COVID-19 shows why united action is needed for more robust international health architecture*, www.who.int/news-room/commentaries/detail/op-ed–covid-19-shows-why-united-action-is-needed-for-more-robust-international-health-architecture.

World Health Organization. (2021c). *COVID-19: Make it the last pandemic. The independent panel for preparedness and response*, https://theindependentpanel.org/wp-content/uploads/2021/05/COVID-19-Make-it-the-Last-Pandemic_final.pdf.

World Health Organization. (2022a). *International health regulations (IHR) – Background*, www.emro.who.int/international-health-regulations/about/background.html.

World Health Organization. (2022b). *Strengthening the global architecture for health emergency preparedness, response, and resilience: White paper for consultation*, www.who.int/publications/m/item/strengthening-the-global-architecture-for-health-emergency-preparedness-response-and-resilience.

World Health Organization. (2022c). *Strengthening WHO preparedness for and response to health Emergencies: Proposal for amendments to the International Health Regulations* (2005), https://apps.who.int/gb/ebwha/pdf_files/WHA75/A75_18-en.pdf.

World Health Organization. (2022d). *Zero draft report of the working group on strengthening WHO preparedness and response to health emergencies to the seventy-fifth World Health Assembly*, https://apps.who.int/gb/wgpr/e/e_wgpr-9.html.

World Health Organization. (2023a). *Zero draft of the WHO CA+ for the consideration of the Intergovernmental Negotiating Body at its fourth meeting WHO convention, agreement or other international instrument on pandemic prevention, preparedness and response*, https://apps.who.int/gb/inb/pdf_files/inb4/A_INB4_3-en.pdf.

World Health Organization. (2023b). *DRAFT Bureau's text of the WHO CA+ WHO convention, agreement or other international instrument on pandemic prevention, preparedness and response*, https://apps.who.int/gb/inb/pdf_files/inb5/A_INB5_6-en.pdf.

Zürn, M. & Checkel, J. (2005). Getting socialized to build bridges: Constructivism and rationalism, Europe and the nation-state. *International Organization*, 59(4), 1045–1079.

Zürn, M. (2016). Historical institutionalism and international relations – strange bedfellows? In T. Rixen, L. A. Viola, & M. Zürn, eds., *Historical Institutionalism and International Relations: Explaining Institutional Development in World Politics*. Oxford: Oxford University Press, pp. 199–228.

Zvobgo, K. & Loken, M. (2020). *Why race matters in international relations*, https://foreignpolicy.com/2020/06/19/why-race-matters-international-relations-ir/.

Zwingel, S. (2016). *Translating International Women's Rights: The CEDAW Convention in Context*. London: Palgrave Macmillan.

Acknowledgements

We thank Rebecca Adler-Nissen, Stephen Brown, Christian Bueger, Alena Drieschova, Ted Hopf, and Vincent Pouliot for generous comments, suggestions, and critical feedback at various stages of the project. We thank Michaela Pedersen-Macnab for her able research assistance. We are also extremely grateful for detailed comments, suggestions, and guidance from two anonymous reviewers and, especially, the series editor, Jeff Checkel. Steven Bernstein would also like to thank the Social Sciences and Humanities Research Council of Canada for generous support of research that contributed to this project.

Cambridge Elements

International Relations

Series Editors

Jon C. W. Pevehouse
University of Wisconsin–Madison

Jon C. W. Pevehouse is the Mary Herman Rubinstein Professor of Political Science and Public Policy at the University of Wisconsin–Madison. He has published numerous books and articles in IR in the fields of international political economy, international organizations, foreign policy analysis, and political methodology. He is a former editor of the leading IR field journal, International Organization.

Tanja A. Börzel
Freie Universität Berlin

Tanja A. Börzel is the Professor of political science and holds the Chair for European Integration at the Otto-Suhr-Institute for Political Science, Freie Universität Berlin. She holds a PhD from the European University Institute, Florence, Italy. She is coordinator of the Research College "The Transformative Power of Europe," as well as the FP7-Collaborative Project "Maximizing the Enlargement Capacity of the European Union" and the H2020 Collaborative Project "The EU and Eastern Partnership Countries: An Inside-Out Analysis and Strategic Assessment." She directs the Jean Monnet Center of Excellence "Europe and its Citizens."

Edward D. Mansfield
University of Pennsylvania

Edward D. Mansfield is the Hum Rosen Professor of Political Science, University of Pennsylvania. He has published well over 100 books and articles in the area of international political economy, international security, and international organizations. He is Director of the Christopher H. Browne Center for International Politics at the University of Pennsylvania and former program co-chair of the American Political Science Association.

Editorial Team

International Relations Theory
Jeffrey T. Checkel, European University Institute, Florence

International Political Economy
Edward D. Mansfield, University of Pennsylvania
Stefanie Walter, University of Zurich

International Security
Jon C. W. Pevehouse, University of Wisconsin–Madison

International Organisations
Tanja A. Börzel, Freie Universität Berlin

About the Series

The Cambridge Elements Series in International Relations publishes original research on key topics in the field. The series includes manuscripts addressing international security, international political economy, international organizations, and international relations.

Cambridge Elements⁼

International Relations

Elements in the Series

Peace in Digital International Relations: Prospects and Limitations
Oliver P. Richmond, Gëzim Visoka and Ioannis Tellidis

Regionalized Governance in the Global South
Brooke Coe and Kathryn Nash

Digital Globalization: Politics, Policy, and a Governance Paradox
Stephen Weymouth

After Hedging: Hard Choices for the Indo-Pacific States between the US and China
Kai He and Huiyun Feng

IMF Lending: Partisanship, Punishment, and Protest
M. Rodwan Abouharb and Bernhard Reinsberg

Building Pathways to Peace: State–Society Relations and Security Sector Reform
Nadine Ansorg and Sabine Kurtenbach

Drones, Force and Law: European Perspectives
David Hastings Dunn and Nicholas J. Wheeler

The Selection and Tenure of Foreign Ministers Around the World
Hanna Bäck, Alejandro Quiroz Flores and Jan Teorell

Lockean Liberalism in International Relations
Alexandru V. Grigorescu and Claudio J. Katz

Tip-toeing through the Tulips with Congress: How Congressional Attention Constrains Covert Action
Dani Kaufmann Nedal and Madison V. Schramm

Social Cues: How the Liberal Community Legitimizes Humanitarian War
Jonathan A. Chu

Norms, Practices, and Social Change in Global Politics
Steven Bernstein, Aarie Glas and Marion Laurence

A full series listing is available at: www.cambridge.org/EIR

For EU product safety concerns, contact us at Calle de José Abascal, 56–1°, 28003 Madrid, Spain or eugpsr@cambridge.org.

www.ingramcontent.com/pod-product-compliance
Lightning Source LLC
LaVergne TN
LVHW020350260326
834688LV00045B/1643